D1799843

MUMMY CASES and INSCRIBED FUNERARY CONES

MUMMY-CASES
and
INSCRIBED FUNERARY CONES

IN THE PETRIE COLLECTION

H. M. Stewart

ARIS & PHILLIPS
BOLCHAZY-CARDUCCI

PUBLISHERS

UK - ISBN 0 85668 312 4
US - ISBN 0 86516 075 9

Printed and published in England by Aris & Phillips Ltd., Teddington House
Warminster, Wiltshire.
Published in the U.S.A. by Bolchazy-Carducci Publishers, 44 Lake Street, Oak Park,
Illinois 60302

CONTENTS

PLATES

PREFACE

Although the coffins and cartonnages in the Petrie Museum form a valuable study collection, the category is perhaps less fully represented than others. Appearances are somewhat distorted here by the fact that many examples from Petrie's own excavations belonged to the Roman Period, which is not covered in the present catalogue. So far as purchased material is concerned, however, any imbalance probably had more to do with financial and customs restrictions[1] than with policy.

Fortunately, the situation regarding funerary cones was different. These appear to have been little valued at the time, and Petrie managed to collect over four hundred examples, which he described summarily in *A Season in Egypt.* The present account, which includes more recent additions, will it is hoped usefully supplement Davies N. de G. & Macadam M.F.L. *Corpus of Inscribed Egyptian Funerary Cones,* the projected commentary volume of which has regrettably been abandoned. Since comprehensive surveys tend to be elusive, it is perhaps only through local inventories that immediate progress is possible.

As in previous catalogues I gratefully acknowledge the help of my colleagues Mrs Barbara Adams and Miss Rosalind Hall, whose identification of objects through Petrie's notes and publications has been crucial. I am also indebted to Mr P. Harrison of the Central Photographic Unit, University College London, for plates 1-3, 12, 17, 18, 20 and 21, and to Dr J. Málek of the Griffith Institute, Ashmolean Museum, Oxford, Dr H. Whitehouse, also of the Ashmolean Museum, and Mr T.G.H. James of the Department of Egyptian Antiquities, British Museum, for their valuable co-operation.

1. See Edwards A.B. *A Thousand Miles up the Nile* (2nd ed.), 451.

BIBLIOGRAPHY AND ABBREVIATIONS

Periodicals

Annales du Service des Antiquités de l'Égypte. Cairo.
Annals of Archaeology and Anthropology. Liverpool.
Archiv Orientální. Prague.
Bulletin de l'Institut français d'Archéologie orientale. Cairo.
Chronique d'Égypte. Brussels.
Journal of Egyptian Archaeology. London.
Jaarbericht Ex Oriente Lux. Leyden.
Kêmi. Paris.
Orientalistische Litteratur-Zeitung. Berlin.
Studien zur altägyptischen Kultur. Hamburg.
Transactions of the International Congress of Orientalists. Leyden.
Zeitschrift für Ägyptische Sprache und Altertumskunde. Leipzig & Berlin.

Books

Aegyptische Inschriften aus den königlichen Museen zu Berlin. 2 vols. Leipzig, 1901-24.
Barta W. *Aufbau und Bedeutung der altägyptischen Opferformel* (Ägyptologische Forschungen 24). Glückstadt, 1968.
Bonnet H. *Reallexikon der ägyptischen Religionsgeschichte.* Berlin, 1952.
Botti G. *Le antichita egiziane del Museo dell' Accademia di Cortona.* Florence, 1955.
Id. *Le Casse di Mummie i Sarcofagi da el Hibeh nel Museo Egizio di Firenze.* Florence, 1958.
Brunner-Traut E. & Brunner H. *Die ägyptische Sammlung der Universität Tübingen.* Mainz, 1981.
Budge E.A.W. *Some account of the Collection of Egyptian Antiquities in the possession of Lady Meux.* London, 1896.
Daressy G. *Recueil de cônes funéraires.* Mémoires publiés par les membres de la Mission archéologique française au Caire, 8, 269 ff. Cairo, 1893.
David R. *The Macclesfield Collection of Egyptian Antiquities.* Warminster, 1980.
Davies N. de G. *The Tombs of Menkheperrasonb etc.* London, 1933.
Davies N. de G. & Gardiner A.H. *The Tomb of Amenemhet.* London, 1915.
Davies N. de G. & Macadam M.F.L. *A Corpus of Inscribed Egyptian Funerary Cones.* Oxford, 1957.
Droste V. von & Schlick-Nolte B. *Museen der Rhein-Main-Region (Corpus Antiquitatum Aegyptiacarum).* Mainz, 1984.
Fabretti A., Rossi F. & Lanzone R.V. *Regio Museo di Torino. Sezione egizia.* Turin, 1931-8.
Gauthier H. *Livre des rois d'Égypte,* 5 vols. Cairo, 1907-17.
Graefe E. *Untersuchungen zur Verwaltung und Geschichte der Institution der Gottesgemahlin des Amun* (Ägyptologische Abhanlungen, Bd. 37). 2 vols. Wiesbaden 1982.
Hayes W.C. *The Scepter of Egypt,* 2 vols. Metropolitan Museum of Art, New York, 1953-9.

Helck W. *Der Einfluss der Militärführer in der 18. ägyptischen Dynastie.* Leipzig, 1939.

Id. *Materialien zur Wirtschaftsgeschichte des Neuen Reiches.* Wiesbaden, 1961-70.

Id. *Zur Verwaltung des Mittleren und Neuen Reiches.* Leyden, 1958.

Helck W., Otto E. & Westendorf W. *Lexikon der Ägyptologie.* Wiesbaden, 1972-.

James T.G.H. *Corpus of Hieroglyphic Inscriptions in the Brooklyn Museum* I. Brooklyn, 1974.

Kees H. *Das Priestertum im ägyptischen Staat.* Leyden, 1953. *Indices u. Nachträge.* 1958.

Leclant J. *Mentouemhat.* Cairo, 1961.

Legrain G. *Répertoire généalogique et onomastique du Musée du Caire.* Cairo, 1908.

Lefebvre G. *Histoire des grands prêtres d'Amon de Karnak.* Paris, 1929.

Luxor Museum of Ancient Egyptian Art. Cairo, American Research Center in Egypt, 1979.

Mogensen M. *Inscriptions hiéroglyphiques du Musée National de Copenhague.* Copenhagen, 1918.

Mond R.L. & Myers O.H. *Temples of Armant.* London, 1940.

Naville E. *Das aegyptische Todtenbuch der XVIII. bis XX. Dynastie.* Einleitung and I-II. Berlin, 1886.

Northampton (Marquess of), Spiegelberg W. & Newberry P.E. *Report of some excavations in the Theban Necropolis.* London, 1908.

Otto E. *Topographie des thebanischen Gaues.* Berlin, 1952.

Petrie W.M.F. *Funeral Furniture of Egypt.* London, 1937, repr. Warminster, 1977.

Id. *Gizeh and Rifeh.* London, 1907.

Id. *Hawara, Biahmu & Arsinoe.* London, 1889.

Id. *Qurneh.* London, 1909.

Id. *A Season in Egypt.* London, 1888.

Petrie W.M.F. & Brunton G. *Sedment,* 2 vols. London, 1921.

Porter B. & Moss R.L. *Topographical Bibliography of Ancient Egyptian Hieroglyphic Texts, Reliefs and Paintings,* 7 vols. (in course of revision). Oxford, 1927 -.

Price F.G. Hilton, *Catalogue of the Egyptian Antiquities in the possession of F.G. Hilton Price.* London, 1897.

Quibell J.E. *The Ramesseum.* London, 1896.

Ranke H. *Die altägyptische Personennamen,* 2 vols. Glückstadt, 1935.

Reiser E. *Der königliche Harim im alten Ägypten und seine Verwaltung.* Vienna, 1972.

Säve-Söderbergh T. *Four Eighteenth Dynasty Tombs (Private Tombs at Thebes* I). Oxford, 1957.

Schmidt V. *Sarcofager, Mumiekister og Mumiehylstre i det gamle Aegypten, Typologisk Atlas.* Copenhagen, 1919.

Schulman A.R. *Military Rank, Title and Organization in the Egyptian New Kingdom.* Münchner Ägyptologische Studien 6. Berlin, 1964.

Spencer P. *The Egyptian Temple, a Lexicographical Study.* London, 1984.

Urk. IV = Steindorff G. *Urkunden des ägyptischen Altertums,* vol. IV: Sethe K. *Urkunden der 18. Dynastie.* Leipzig, 1914. Continued by Helck W. Berlin, 1955-61.

Wb. = Erman A. & Grapow H. *Wörterbuch der ägyptischen Sprach,* 5 vols. Leipzig, 1926-31.

MUMMY - CASES

MUMMY-CASES

Surprisingly, when one considers the prominence of mummy-cases in collections of Egyptian antiquities, the literature on their development is very meagre, and relatively few examples have been published in detail. The latter fact is perhaps due in part to difficulties in the copying of decoration from surfaces which are in relief; where these are covered with shiny varnish which has darkened with age, photography too may have problems. The present collection is a modest one in which the assortment of styles is too limited to form the basis of a developmental study. It does, however, offer a fair sample of the chief categories, which will be treated in roughly chronological order. The selection described ranges from Dynasty XI to the Ptolemaic Period, but with the strongest concentration on the Late Period, when as a result of increasing tomb-robbery the elaborately decorated tomb was abandoned and much of its iconography transferred to the mummy-case[1]. Some fragmentary material, chiefly Ptolemaic cartonnage, in need of laboratory treatment has had to be omitted - with present resources the completion of this is still remote - but parts of canopic and shabti boxes have been included, which are related to the present theme.

1. See Niwinski A. 'Sarg NR - SpZt' in Helck et al. *Lexikon der Ägyptologie.*

CARTONNAGE MUMMY MASK (UC 31377)
Plate 1

Painted linen cartonnage.
Height 38.2 cm., width 20.0 cm.
Possibly from Sedment, tomb 2101(?).
Dynasty XI.

Mask of a bearded man, his hair having lappets (broken off at the bottom edge) which leave the ears uncovered. His features are well defined except for the eyes, which are merely painted, and he wears a broad collar consisting of plain concentric strands, of which the inner ones remain. Colours used are: skin light ochre; hair, eyebrows and lids black; beard and moustache blue; collar red, green (?), white and black. As was common at that period, the rest of the body was bandaged only.[1]

Bibliography: Petrie & Brunton, *Sedment* I, 10 ('plaster mask with blue moustache and beard'), pl. 39 (tomb register); Bourriau J. in *JEA* 69 (1983), 146 (331).

Note: 1. See Petrie & Brunton, op. cit. I; 6; Hayes, *Scepter* I, 303 ff.

2. SIDE OF A RECTANGULAR COFFIN (UC 38036)
Plate 2

Wood with painted decoration.
Two adjoining fragments, combined length 1.74 m., height 30 cm., thickness 3 cm.
Provenance unknown.
Middle Kingdom - early Dynasty XVIII.

Part of a rectangular coffin of a type prevalent during the Middle Kingdom, when it commonly symbolised a dwelling-house decorated in palace-facade style with the addition of eyes painted on the left (east) side at the head end.[1] The board, divided in two by a modern saw-cut, has painted false-doors alternating with chequered panels, the part below the rim being decorated with a block border which continues vertically down the left end, the right end having been lost. The bottom edge is badly eroded, but in the thickness rectangular mortises remain for the attachment of the base. Colours used are as follows. False-doors: dark green, light green and red areas each framed by white bands. Chequered panels: blue, red, light green and white squares, the last-named having central red spots. The colours in the panels run diagonally. Block border: dark green, light green, yellow and red segments with horizontal bands below in light green, yellow and red.

Note: 1. See Hayes, *Scepter* I, 312 ff.

3. FRAGMENT OF A RECTANGULAR COFFIN (UC 38046)
Plate 2

Wood with painted decoration.
Length 43.0 cm., height 14.0 cm.
From Rifeh.
Dynasty XII.

Upper corner from the side of a rectangular coffin showing part of a surrounding block border within which is the beginning of a *ḥtp-dỉ-nsw* prayer invoking Geb, written in multicoloured hieroglyphs. Below it is a horizontal white band decorated with vertical green lines, presumably part of a panel in a palace-facade design. The general background is yellow with the block border in black, white and red, and the hieroglyphs in black, white, green, red and brown with green dividers. Vertical guide-lines in red mark the widths of the hieroglyphs. While the decorated surface is well preserved, the thickness has been lost.

Bibliography: cf. Petrie, *Gizeh and Rifeh,* 12 f.

4. ANTHROPOID COFFIN (UC 8899)
Plates 3-8

Wood covered with gesso, painted and varnished.
Lid: length 189.8 cm., breadth 68.6 cm.
Base: length 189.0 cm., breadth 53.2 cm.
Presumably from Thebes. Formerly in the Wellcome Collection.
Late Dynasty XXI.

The coffin is of typical late Dynasty XXI style with crowded detail on a yellow ground, very large decorated collar, and a frieze of uraei and ostrich plumes round the sides under the rim.[1] Some discrepancies in the modelling of the lid and the base, and in the colours used in their decoration suggest that the coffin may have been provided with a new lid and re-used, although probably not more than a generation later.[2] (Correspondence of the mortises in both parts confirms that they are indeed a pair.) The absence of an owner's name indicates that the case was mass-produced, and did not belong to a person of very high rank.

THE LID (pls. 3, 4). On the outside a male figure is represented with yellow complexion (the ground colour of the case). He wears a striped black-and-yellow wig bound by a patterned fillet, the lappets leaving the ears exposed. There is no trace of a beard. The shoulders are covered by a decorated collar extending to waist level and crossed by two red straps with yellow ends. The hands, attached separately, hold short batons of oval cross-section. Spread across the lid below the waist are two winged sun-disks and a winged scarab, these being flanked by two winged cobras representing the goddess Edjo. Various symbols fill the interstices. They include the buckle of Isis, a cartouche (illegible), *djed*-pillars, *wedjat*-eyes and *ba*-birds. In columns from the knees downward are two coiled Edjo serpents flanked by rows of uraei and two mummiform gods facing outward. The interior of the lid is undecorated.

THE BASE (pls. 5-8). The outside is heavily decorated along the sides, but left blank at the ends. Below the rim is a frieze of alternating uraei and ostrich plumes, the remainder of the sides being occupied by scenes in panels, separated by double columns of inscription. These repeat the formulae 'Revered by Osiris, lord of eternity, foremost in the West' and 'Revered by Isis, the great one, mother of the god, mistress of the house' except between panels 14 and 17, where 'Revered by Re-Harakhti-Atum, lord of the Two Lands' is substituted for one or the other in turn of the two previous formulae.

The subjects of the panels are as follows.

Left side (pl. 5). 1. Osiris seated before an offering-table. 2. The *ba*-bird adoring a deity. 3-4. Two symmetrical scenes showing Anubis, 'foremost in the divine booth' seated before an offering-table. Between the two scenes is a large *kherp*-sceptre (cf. panels 12-13). 5. The deceased, described as 'the living god', standing before an offering-table. 6. Isis standing before an offering-table. 7. The *ba*-bird adoring Osiris and Isis. 8. A heaped offering-table. 9. Hathor, 'mistress of Dendera' as a cow emerging from the western mountain, on which stands a tomb-chapel.

Right side (pl. 6) 10. Re-Harakhti as a falcon with solar disk under a canopy. He treads a serpent beneath his feet, and is protected by a winged *wedjat*-eye. 11. A mummy figure of the deceased stands under a canopy before a shrine and an offering-table, while the goddess Nekhbet as a vulture holds the *ankh*-symbol to his nostrils. 12-13. Two symmetrical scenes showing Osiris enthroned on a dais beneath a canopy. In both scenes he wears the solar disk on his head and has an offering-table before him. Between the scenes is a large *kherp*-sceptre. 14. The deceased as Osiris seated under a canopy before an offering-table. 15. Anubis standing before an offering table. 16. Isis standing before an offering-table. 17. The *ba*-bird adoring the four sons of Horus, all human-headed, who stand on a lotus-flower. 18. The *ba*-bird receiving water from Hathor (?), goddess of the sycamore tree (c.f. no.17, pl. 22). This scene is much damaged.

Interior (pls. 7,8). The floor of the case is occupied by the figure of Amentet,[3] goddess of the West, of whom little remains but the head and shoulders. Facing her name above is a cobra resting on the sky-symbol. On the sides of the interior a *ba*-bird in face view occupies the head end, flanked by two serpents with the *ankh*-symbol. Both sides have symmetrical scenes of identical content, each with three registers of three mummiform deities facing outward. Those at the top are falcon-, human- and ape-headed, those in the middle human-, serpent- and ape (?)-headed, and at the bottom jackal- and human-headed, the third figure on both sides being lost. Only the jackal-headed god, 'Anubis, lord of the sacred land' is named, the top register having simply 'the great god, lord of the West', and the middle one 'the great god, lord of dread.' Presumably the other figures include the four sons of Horus.

The colours used are red, blue (rendered dark green by the varnish), light green, black and white on a yellow ground. Light green is, however, absent from the lid. The case has suffered extensive damage by water.

Notes: 1. See Niwinski A. 'Sarg NR - SpZt' in Helck et al. *Lexikon der Ägyptologie*. 2. I owe this observation to Dr Niwinski. 3. Cf. Schmidt, *Sarcofager*, nos. 1014, 1178, 1239.

5. PART OF A COFFIN OF AMENEMOPET (UC 15703)
Plates 9, 10

Wood covered with linen cartonnage, painted and varnished.
Length 34 cm., depth 45 cm., thickness 6 cm.
Probably from Deir el-Bahri.[1] Formerly in the Amelia Edwards Collection.
Dynasty XXI.

This fragment of an anthropoid coffin belonged to the head end as is indicated on the inner surface by the *ba*-bird with spread wings, which often occupied that position during Dynasty XXI (cf. pl.7). The end, which is rounded, had been made in dowelled sections, of which the present piece is one.

Exterior (pl. 9). The blank area on the left was at the top of the head. Below the rim on the right is part of a frieze of uraei with sun-disks, which commonly adorned the sides at this period. A single line of text within block borders below this mentions 'Re-Harakhti-Atum, lord of the Two Lands and of Thebes.' In the main register are seated figures named as '['Imn-m-ipt], son of 'Ikfy[2], justified, and his wife, mistress of the house, *T3-nt-di-Hnsw*, justified.' The remainder of the columns have conventional prayers to Osiris, /Isis/, Hathor and Anubis for funerary offerings. A further prayer to /Osiris/ occupies the line below. Along the bottom is a row of *djed*-symbols in pairs, alternating with the buckle of Isis.

Interior (pl. 10). The *ba*-bird with spread wings, holding aloft the rising sun symbol, originally occupied the middle of the arched head end. At right angles to this are figures and texts which continued vertically along the side walls. In the cartouche below the *ba*-bird is the name 'Amenophis the favourite (of Amun)', which related to the cult of the deified Amenophis I, the founder of the Theban royal necropolis.[3] Presumably a figure of that king was represented on the floor of the coffin. Near the top of the arch is the vulture of Nekhbet standing on the 'gold' symbol. Beneath are traces of a solar disk with uraeus, which probably belonged to Re-Harakhti, to whom the deceased is shown addressing a prayer: 'Adoration of Re-Harakhti, doing obeisance to his Ennead, by the Osiris, *'Imn-m-ipt*, justified.'

7

The ground colour of the coffin, both outside and inside, is yellow. On the outside the inscriptions are in blue and red with blue dividers, and the outlines of the figures are in red. On the inside the inscriptions, again in blue and red, are on white backgrounds with other details in red, green, blue, black and white.

Bibliography: Edwards A. in *Transactions of the 6th International Congress of Orientalists* (1883), pt. 4, sect. 3, 167 ff.; Petrie, *Funeral Furniture*, 23 (531); Porter & Moss, *Top. Bibl.* I², 666.

Notes: 1. Amelia Edwards stated (op. cit.) that the fragment, presented to her by the British Consular Agent at Thebes, came 'in all probability' from the cache at Deir el-Bahri. 2. Cf. Ranke, *Personennamen* I, 48(13). 3. See Černý in *BIFAO* 27 (1927), 168; cf. UC 14212 in Stewart, *Egyptian Stelae* I, 47, pl. 38(2).

6. FRAGMENT OF AN ANTHROPOID COFFIN (UC 29809)
Plate 11

Wood covered with gesso, painted and varnished.
Height 11.7 cm., width 37 cm.
From tomb-chapel 125,[1] Ramesseum, Thebes.
Dynasty XXI - XXII.

The fragment, belonging to the central area of the lid, shows parts of four columns of hieroglyphs which contain a *ḥtp-dỉ-nsw* prayer invoking Re-Harakhti and /Osiris/ on behalf of the owner (name lost). On both sides are portions of symmetrical scenes each showing two deities seated before an offering-table. These are almost certainly the four sons of Horus, for the name *Dwȝ-[mwt.f]* appears by the jackal-headed figure on the left. The background is yellow, and the figures and hieroglyphs are red, yellow and blue (made dark green by the varnish), all painted on a thin layer of gesso. Three dowels penetrate the surface diagonally towards the upper edge.

Bibliography: Quibell, *Ramesseum*, 9, 12 (general notes only).

Note: 1. Not to be confused with the Theban tomb number.

7.   ANTHROPOID COFFIN OF NAIRTESINEFER (UC 14230)
Plates 12-16

Wood covered with linen cartonnage and gesso, painted and varnished. The lid and the base were carved from single baulks and not constructed.
Length 1.76 m., breadth 47.5 cm.
Probably from Thebes. Presented to University College before 1890.
Late Dynasty XXII (?).

Lid, exterior (pls. 12,13). The figure represented, that of a woman, has a plain coiffure bound by a fillet which leaves the ears uncovered. She wears a broad, decorated collar, below which is a ram-headed falcon with sun-disk and outspread wings, commonly replacing the goddess Nut here at this period.[1] Below this motif is a succession of registers.

(a)   The deceased adoring Osiris and other mummiform deities (unnamed), which appear to include the four sons of Horus.

(b)   The judgement scene with the deceased being led by Thoth before a tribunal of gods headed by Osiris.

(c)   The mummy lying on its bier flanked by falcons with sun-disks on their heads. In columns on each side of the bier the deceased is named: 'the Osiris, mistress of the house, *N3-ỉr(t)-3st-nfr* (henceforth referred to as *N*), justified.'

(d)   An inscription in 13 columns: 'Words spoken by *N*, justified, daughter of the prophet (*ḥm-ntr*) of Monthu[2], lord of Thebes, *B3s3*, justified, son of the similarly titled *P3-dỉ-3st*, justified, her mother being the mistress of the house, *T3-ʿ3w*, justified, daughter of the beloved of the god, the hour-watcher (*wnwty*) in Karnak, *Ỉw.f-n-'Imn*, justified, son of the similarly titled *Ḏd-Mntw-ỉ(w.f)-ʿnḫ*, justified. Hail, Osiris, bull of the west, the great god who is in . . . (text unfinished).

(e)   A group of deities and/or demons seated on both sides of the Abydos fetish. Inscribed in two columns: 'Words spoken by *N*, daughter of the god's-father (*ỉt-ntr*), the offerer (*ḥnk-nw*?)[3] in Thebes, *B3s3*, justified.'

(f)   Five columns beginning: 'Words spoken by the Osiris *[N]* . . . ' (remainder lost). A crouching jackal, the symbol of Wepwawet, faces the front on both sides of the feet.

Lid, interior (pl. 15). At the head end stands a figure of Nut in face view holding aloft the sun-disk. Facing her are four apes (*ỉmyw-ḥtt*) 'adoring the god four times.' The inscription below in nine columns and two lines derives from Chapter 68 of the Book of the Dead. 'Words spoken by *N*, justified. The doors of heaven are opened for the Osiris *N*. The doors of the earth are opened for *N*. The door-bolts of Geb are opened for *N*, justified. The sky-windows[4] are opened for *N*. He who bound her arm releases her. *N*, justified. His (erron. her) arm is drawn from her to the ground.[5] The mouth of the Pelican[6] is opened, and the mouth is opened for *N*. The mouth of the Pelican is opened, and *N* goes forth by day to all the places her heart desires. Words spoken by

Osiris. May he grant invocation-offerings of bread, beer, oxen, fowl, incense, clothing and all good and pure things and all pleasant things to *N*, justified.' In the next register the *ba*-bird is shown hovering over the mummy on its bier. Facing this scene on both sides are Isis, 'mother of the god, who protects the mistress', and Nephthys, 'sister of the god, who protects *N*', both kneeling on 'gold' symbols. There follow two lines of inscription: 'Words spoken by *N*, daughter of the beloved of the god, the offerer in Thebes, *B3s3*.'

In seven columns and one line below is a version of Chapter 56 of the Book of the Dead. 'O Atum, mayst thou give the sweet breath which is in thy nostrils to *N*. It is she who occupies the throne which is in the midst of Hermopolis. He has guarded[7] the egg[8] of the great cackler. If it flourishes, *N* flourishes, and vice versa. If it lives, *N* lives, and vice versa. If it breathes air, *N* breathes air, and vice versa. *N*, justified, lady of reverence.'

Base, exterior (pl. 14). The most prominent feature is the large, centrally placed *djed*-symbol crowned with ostrich plumes, sun-disk and ram's horns. Duplicated on both sides are pairs of squatting gods, unnamed, but presumably the four sons of Horus. In columns between the rows are virtually identical captions: 'Words spoken by *N*, justified, lady of reverence, daughter of the god's-father, offerer in Thebes, *B3s3*, justified, revered, son of the similarly titled *P3-dĩ-3st*, her mother being the mistress *T3-ꜥ3w*, justified. Hail, *[Osiris]* ... bull of the West.'

Base, interior (pl. 16). At the head is the raying sun with uraei on which hang *ankh*-symbols. The inscription below is divided into five sections written alternately horizontally and vertically, an arrangement which, since the text is continuous, is purely decorative. The contents derive in part from Chapter 26 of the Book of the Dead. 'Words spoken by *N*, justified, daughter of the god's-father of Amun, the offerer in Thebes, *B3s3*, justified, her mother being the mistress of the house, *T3-ꜥ3w*, justified, daughter of the god's-father of Amen-Re, king of the gods, *'Iw-f-n-'Imn*, justified. Words spoken. The mind (*ĩb*) of *N* is given to her in the house of minds, and her heart (*h3ty*) to her in the house of hearts. The mind of *N* belongs to her, and she is content with it. She has not eaten the offering-cake of Osiris on yonder[9] eastern side of *G3yt*.[10] The *hwht*-ship sails upstream. May *N* not go down. The daughter of the god's-father of Amun, the offerer in Thebes, *B3s3*, justified, son of the god's-father of Amun, offerer in Thebes, *P3-dĩ-3st*, justified, son of the similarly titled *B3s3*, justified, revered by Osiris.'

On both sides of the interior are almost identical columns of text: 'Words spoken by *N*, justified, daughter of the god's-father of Amun, the offerer in Thebes, *B3s3*, justified, revered by the great god.' At the bottom end is the disk of the setting sun (not illustrated).

The background colour of the decoration is white, the complexion of the figure yellow and the hair black. The hieroglyphs are blue, mostly with red dividers, and the remaining decoration is in red, blue (now dark green) and yellow. Since the varnish on the outside has darkened considerably, the colour values have altered, and much of the painted detail

10

has been obscured. The lid was attached in the usual way with rectangular pegs secured by dowels through the thickness of the coffin sides.

Bibliography: Petrie, *Funeral Furniture*, 22 f.(530); Porter & Moss, *Top. Bibl.* I², 830; Kelly V. *Some initial steps in the technological analysis and conservation of an Egyptian mummy-case* (unpublished thesis, Institute of Archaeology, University of London, 1979).

Notes: 1. Niwinski A. 'Sarg NR - SpZt' in Helck et al. *Lexikon der Ägyptologie.* 2. There appears to be no genealogical connection with the priests of Monthu buried at Deir el-Bahri; see Porter & Moss, op. cit. I², 643 ff. 3. *Wb.* III, 118. 4. *Ptr.ty: Wb.* I, 565. 5. The oddly placed break at the foot of col. 7 suggests that the scribe may have been copying from a damaged or partly illegible text. 6. The word *ḥnt* has the 'pelican' determinative in most copies (cf. also Coffin Texts, spell 225), although it is absent here. There seems, however, to have been some uncertainty about the meaning of the word, for it is sometimes written with the 'canal' determinative (Naville, *Todtenbuch* II, 144, cf. *Wb.* III, 105). On the pelican in Egyptian mythology see Otto E. in *Studies presented to David Moore Robinson* (St. Louis, Miss. 1951), 215 ff. 7. While the pronoun suggests Atum, parallel texts make the deceased the subject. The verb should be read as *sꜣw*. 8. A creation myth; see Bonnet, *Reallexikon*, 162 f. 9. For *ps* read *pf.* 10. A place in the Netherworld; see *Wb.* IV, 150(17).

8. CARTONNAGE OF NESPAUTITAWY (UC 16022, 38039)
Plates 17, 18

Painted linen cartonnage.
Two fragments: upper (UC 38039, height 34.6 cm., width 18.5 cm.;
lower (UC 16022), height 40 cm., width 27 cm.
Probably from the Ramesseum area at Thebes. Formerly in the Amelia Edwards Collection.
Dynasty XXII or later.

These two pieces are almost certainly from the same cartonnage and probably contiguous, although the edges are too abraded to provide a clear join — the facts that the fragments both belong to the Edwards Collection (quite a small one), are identical in colour scheme, notably in the banded decoration, and have the same inscriptional style and column width show a correspondence too strong to be coincidental.

They contain parts of panelled registers from the right side of the cartonnage, the upper register (pl. 17) showing a winged goddess, presumably Isis, with sun-disk on her head, and the lower register Horus, 'the Behdetite, the great god, lord of heaven.' Below each of these is part of a line of inscription: (a) '. . . / Anubis, foremost in/ the divine booth. May he grant offerings . . .', (b) '. . . the mighty one of heaven (i.e. Isis), who gives protection to her lord every day.' In a panel at the bottom at right-angles to the other scenes is a squatting, crocodile-headed demon.

11

On the left of the lower fragment (pl. 18) is a panel containing the emblem of Nefertem, a plumed lotus rising from a *šn*-ring. The central column of inscription reads: '(a) . . . all good and pure offerings, all things good, sweet and pleasant on the offering-table (in) thousands. The Osiris, keeper of the funerary offerings (*sȝw*[1] *prt-ḫrw*) . . .[2] (b) and of the things pertaining to[3] the divine votaress of Amun (*dwȝt-ntr 'Imn*), *Ns-pȝwty-tȝwy*[4], son of the keeper of the treasure-houses (*sȝw prw-ḥḏ*) and of the things pertaining to the divine votaress of Amun, *Ns-pȝ-kȝ-swty* . . .'

The background colour is orange except in the Nefertem panel, where it is white. Other colours used are light green (notably the goddess's skin), blue (now dark green), yellow and red.

Bibliography: (UC 16022 only) Petrie, *Funeral Furniture*, 21(506); Porter & Moss, *Top. Bibl.* I², 681; Graefe, *Untersuchungen zur Verwaltung und Geschichte der Institution der Gottesgemahlin des Amun* I, 229 f., Taf. 25a, 11*; II, 108.

Notes: 1. The spelling confirms that the reading of the same word in the lower fragment is *sȝw* and not *iry* (see Graefe, op. cit I, 230). 2. Possibly nothing has been lost here. 3. As Graefe notes, this form of expression is unusual. 4. The fuller context of the name would seem to resolve doubts expressed by Graefe about the ownership of the cartonnage.

9.   CARTONNAGE OF HARSIESI (UC 16023)
Plate 11

Painted linen cartonnage.
Height 12 cm., breadth 11.5 cm.
From the Ramesseum area at Thebes.
Dynasty XXII.

Fragment from the cartonnage of a fourth prophet of Amun (*ḥm-ntr 4-nw 'Imn*),*Ḥr-sȝ-ȝst*. The man's name and title   are framed in a pattern of horizontal chevrons, below which are the head and raised arm of a goddess, presumably a winged Isis. The skin of the figure is green, the hair blue, tied by a red fillet, and the background of the scene white. The inscription and chevrons are on a yellow ground, the chevrons being green, blue and red in turn.

Bibliography: Petrie, *Funerary Furniture,* 21(508); Porter & Moss, *Top. Bibl.* I², 681.

10. FRAGMENT OF CARTONNAGE (UC 29805)
Plate 11

Painted linen cartonnage.
Height 8.7 cm., width 8 cm.
From tomb-chapel 145[1], Ramesseum, Thebes.
Dynasty XXII.

The head and raised arm of a goddess, probably Isis, wearing the uraeus, with part of a wing belonging to a central figure, possibly Nut. (Scenes showing Nut flanked by Isis and Nephthys often appeared below the decorated collar.) The skin of the goddess is cream coloured, her robe green and blue, the wing blue on red, and the background white.

Bibliography: Quibell, *Ramesseum*, 9, 12 (general notes only).

Note: 1. Not to be confused with the Theban tomb number.

11. FRAGMENT OF CARTONNAGE (UC 29806)
Plate 11

Painted linen cartonnage.
Height 18.3 cm., width 6.7 cm.
From tomb-chapel 145, Ramesseum, Thebes.
Dynasty XXII.

Part of a wing of 'Isis of Chemmis' is shown, coloured dark green, red and yellow with some spotted blue. The background is white except in the inscription, which is dark green on yellow. The horizontal bands above are red and dark green on yellow. Part of a *wedjat*-eye remains at the bottom left.

Bibliography: Quibell, *Ramesseum,* 9, 12 (general notes only).

12. FRAGMENT OF CARTONNAGE (UC 38040)
Plate 11

Painted linen cartonnage.
Height 25 cm., width 17 cm.
Provenance unknown.
Late Period.

The fragment contains a central column of inscription flanked by the wings of two goddesses, probably Isis and Nephthys, to one of whom belonged the feet on the left. The inscription reads: '. . . / priestess of/ A/me/n-Re(?)[1] of the fourth phyle (ḥr s3 4-nw), [T] 3-dˆit-nb(t)-ḥnw(?)'.[2] The inscription is in black on a yellow ground, the background of the goddess on the left being white, her feet yellow, and the wings blue on red with some green.

Notes: 1. The absence of the stroke after the sun symbol might suggest the name A/te/n, but such an occurrence at this period would be very surprising. 2. Cf. Ranke, *Personennamen* I, 373(17), 374(15).

13. FRAGMENT OF CARTONNAGE (UC 38041)
Plate 11

Painted linen cartonnage.
Height 14.5 cm., width 8 cm.
Provenance unknown.
Late Period.

The fragment shows two of the four sons of Horus, Imset and Hepy (the latter ape-headed), who are named in the captions above. The painting is on a white ground, and the faces of the two gods are coloured green and red respectively. Blue is used for the hair of Imset, yellow for the collars of both figures, and red for the torsos. The inscription is in black on a yellow ground, and the horizontal bands above are red and green.

14. CARTONNAGE OF PEDIAMUN-NESUTTAWY (UC 38038)
Plate 19

Unpainted linen cartonnage with incised decoration.
Four fragments: (A) height 27.5 cm., width 18.5 cm., (B) height 28 cm., width 17 cm., (C) height 30.5 cm., width 17 cm., (D) height 10.5 cm., width 10 cm.
Probably from Thebes. Previously in the Amelia Edwards Collection.
Late Period.

These fragments of cartonnage are mainly from the left side of the body, covering the area from the chest to the upper part of the feet, where the casing turns outwards. An inward curve in fragment B marks the position of the knees. At the top (A) is part of a register which includes a *ba*-bird before a bread-offering. The line of inscription below reads: ' . . . door / keeper? / (/ ˆiry/-ꜥ3) in the temple of Karnak, overseer of craftsmen (ˆimy-r ḥmwt) in the temple of Amun . . .' The wing and left arm belonged to a central figure of Nut, before whom were represented the four sons of Horus, Qebhsenuef being missing. (The names of Hepy and Duamutef have been transposed by the scribe.) On the right are two columns of inscription which were probably separated from those in the fragment below by another horizontal line of text. The upper pair of columns reads: '. . . those who are caused to cross (the sky) in the company of the righteous ones. Thou art united with the assessors . . . of Osiris. The Osiris, god's-father (*ỉt-ntr*), beloved of the god, *Pȝ-dỉ-'Imn-nswt-tȝwy* . . .' In the next register (B) is another mummiform god before whom are two columns of text: '. . . the realm of the dead. Thou art received in a goodly burial, made for . . . Thy body is protected forever and ever. The Osiris, god's-father, beloved of the god . . .' In the line below is a further caption: '. . . overseer of craftsmen in the temple of Amun, *Pywy*, justified.' The lowest fragment (C) shows Anubis with his right arm raised. Above him is inscribed: 'Anubis, foremost in the divine booth, the great god, who is skilled of counsel in the necropolis. I lay my hand upon him who is in . . .' In two columns in front is a caption belonging to another scene: 'She (a goddess) guards and protects the Osiris, god's-father, beloved of the god, *Pȝ-dỉ-'Imn-nswt-tȝwy*, justified with Osiris.' Two further columns at the left edge of the fragment are much abraded, and yield little but the title 'god's-father.' At the bottom are the remains of two more lines reading: 'The Osiris, god's-father, beloved of the god, *Pȝ-dỉ-*. . .' and 'Hathor, mistress of the West (?)' A small unplaced fragment (D) probably belonged to the middle register. It contains a foot at the top edge, matching in scale the foot of the figure in that register, and has below it a line of text and three columns, all of similar dimensions to the texts they would continue. The line reads: '. . . the temple of Karnak, *Pȝ-dỉ-'Imn-nswt-tȝwy* . . .' and the columns: 'Words spoken by . . . Thou hast . . . the throne . . . *Pȝ-[dỉ-]'Imn-nswt-tȝwy* . . .

15. LID OF AN ANTHROPOID COFFIN (UC 36213)
Plate 20

Wood covered with gesso and painted.
Length 1.88 m., breadth 51.8 cm.
Provenance unknown.
Ptolemaic(?).

The face appears to be that of a woman wearing a wig which covers the ears, and bearing on her forehead a winged black scarab, the wings of which merge with the decoration of the headdress.[1] Round her neck is a broad, decorated collar, below which the rest of the lid is plain except for a single column of hieroglyphs enclosed in a frame upon which crouches the figure of Anubis. A wide split down the middle of the column has resulted in extensive loss of the text, a *ḥtp-dỉ-nsw* prayer[2] with no name preserved. Apart from the carved headpiece the main area of the lid is flat, some depth having been provided by a rim of 4 cm. thickness dowelled to the underside, and containing the sawn-off ends of pegs which attached the lid to the base. The ground colour of the lid is yellow, the face red with eyes in black and white. The headdress and collar are in blue and red, and the inscription is in black on a ground which is white within the frame.

Notes: 1. Cf. Botti, *Le Casse di Mummie . . . Firenze*, pls. 32(1), 48. A similar style of headdress appears also on men, see Budge, *Egyptian Antiquities in the possession of Lady Meux*, frontispiece. 2. What remains shows some affinity with Barta, *Opferformel*, 213 (25).

16. CARTONNAGE MUMMY MASK (UC 28117)
Plate 21

Papyrus cartonnage, painted and gilded.
Height 49 cm.
From Hawara (?).[1]
Ptolemaic.

The mask covered the head from the chest to below the nape of the neck, and also part of the shoulders. The face, apparently that of a woman, is gilded, and the rest of the surface decorated with painted figures and designs arranged symmetrically. On both sides of the ears are Horus-falcons, and on the lappets panels showing (a) the mummy of the deceased standing before the enthroned Osiris and (b) squatting figures of gods. The top of the head bears a winged scarab, and at the back, suspended from the headband, are uraei wearing the crowns of Upper and Lower Egypt. Flanking the uraei are winged goddesses with sun-disks on their heads, and below is a standing mummy figure, presumably of the deceased. The colours used are gold, red, green, yellow, blue, brown and black on a buff ground (perhaps originally white). The piece is well preserved but somewhat crushed.

Bibliography: Petrie, *Funeral Furniture*, 18 (351?).

Note: 1. Cf. Petrie, *Hawara, Biahmu & Arsinoe,* pl. 9(1).

17. PAINTED CASKET OF NEFERTIRY (UC 38042)
Plate 22

Wood with painted decoration.
Side only: length 29.5 cm., height 22.5 cm., thickness 1.2 cm.
From Thebes.
Dynasty XIX.

The front is preserved of a box bearing a painted representation of the owner, 'the Osiris, mistress of the house, singer (*šmʿyt*) of Amun, *Nfrt-îry* justified, in peace (in) the west of Thebes.' She is shown kneeling, dressed in a white, pleated robe, and has long, curled hair reaching to waist level. Before her is the figure of a goddess, who dispenses water and other offerings from a sycamore tree, and who is described as 'Nut, the great one, who bore all the gods.' (Elsewhere the role of tree-goddess often belonged to Hathor). Two round knobs served to secure the lid, and dowels inserted diagonally at each end connected the adjacent sides. The background colour is yellow, the hieroglyphs are black with red dividers, and the complexions of the two figures pink. The hair of the woman is black and of the goddess blue, the sycamore fruits[1] and the skirt of the goddess are red, and the decorative frieze at the top is in green, blue and red.

Note: 1. The Egyptian sycamore is a species of fig-tree.

18. SHABTI BOX OF BASA (UC 38043)
Plate 23

Wood with painted decoration.
Length 26.4 cm., breadth 11 cm., height 20 cm.
Probably from Thebes. Formerly in the Wellcome Collection, where it was acquired in 1929 from a private collector.
Dynasty XXV or later.

A white-painted wooden box, presumably intended to hold shabtis - when acquired by the Wellcome Collection it contained over 200 very crudely modelled, uninscribed examples in green-painted pottery, each about 4 cm. long, which may or may not have belonged to it. The ends of the box are rounded at the top like the Lower Egyptian shrine, on which many such boxes were modelled.[1] Round the sides is a painted inscription: 'Words spoken by the Osiris[2], priest (w^{c}b) of Amun[3], B3s3 the younger, justified, son of S3ny3, justified, the revered one.[4] The lid bears the painting of a sailing ship in yellow and red, the water being coloured blue. The hieroglyphs are in blue with red dividers. Dowels, inserted diagonally, fixed the sides and the lid.

Notes: 1. For an example of similar form and decoration see Mogensen, *Inscriptions hieroglyphiques*, 84, pl. 26, fig. 44. 2. On the writing of Osiris as an indication of the date see Leahy A. in *Studien zur altag. Kultur* 7 (1979), 141 ff. 3. Underlying traces of B3s3 show that in the first draft the word Amun had been omitted. 4. 'Im3(ḫw).

19. BOX LID OF TAWEHERT (UC 16403)
Plate 24

Wood with painted decoration.
Length 26 cm., breadth (incomplete) 16.5 cm., thickness 1.8 cm. tapering to 1.2 cm.
Probably from Thebes. Formerly in Amelia Edwards Collection.
Late Period.

The fragment, which belongs to the lid of a box, probably canopic[1], is rounded on the upper front edge, and tapers in thickness from front to rear as in a shrine roof. A central column of hieroglyphs reads: 'Words spoken by the Osiris *T3-whr(t)*, justified, daughter of *P3-di̯-'Imn-nb-nswt-t3wy*[2], justified, born of the mistress of the house, *T3-srit̯-i̯ʿḥ*, justified.' On both sides of the inscription are symmetrical panels showing Anubis crouching on his shrine, these representations, flanked by parallel stripes, being turned at right-angles to the inscription. Part of the right panel is missing, some dowel holes remaining in the edge. Diagonally cut dowel holes in the edge of the lid served to secure it.

The colours used are as follows: the borders of the lid red, the background of the inscription yellow, and of the Anubis panel white, Anubis black, the shrine yellow with red door, and the stripes green and red.

Bibliography: Petrie, *Funeral Furniture,* 23(533), where the piece is described as the foot of a coffin.

Notes: 1. Cf. *Catalogue, Luxor Museum*, no. 263, fig. 141. 2. For the writing of *nswt t3wy* see *Wb.* II, 327.

INDEXES

1. U.C. Registration Numbers

2. Personal names

3. Titles

4. Divinities

Amenophis I (deified), 5.
Amentet, 4.
Amun/Amen-Re, 7,8,9,12,14,17,18.
Anubis, 4,5,8 14,19.
Atum, 4,5,7.
Edjo, 4.
Geb, 3.
Hathor, 4,5,14,17.
Horus, 8,16.
Horus, sons of, 4,6,7,13,14.
Isis, 4,5,7,12.
Monthu, 7.
Nefertem, 8.
Nekhbet, 4.
Nephthys, 7,10,12.
Nut, 7,10,14,17.
Osiris, 4,5,7,8,14,16.
Re-Harakhti, 4,5,6.
Wepwawet, 7.

5. Provenances

Hawara, 16.
Rifeh, 3.
Sedment, 1.
Thebes, 4-11,14,17,18,19.

FUNERARY CONES

FUNERARY CONES

The pottery cones described here are of the type usually stamped with the owner's name on the butt and embedded in horizontal rows in the facades of private tombs.[1] They are mainly of Dynasty XVIII date, but also occur sporadically during Dynasties XI to XXVI. Apart from a few found as far afield as Aniba, and generally uninscribed, the great majority, including all the present examples, are from the Theban necropolis, several being assignable to known tombs.

Petrie's cones were collected by him mainly from dealers at Luxor[2], and he described how he reduced the bulk by sawing or breaking off the stamped ends, which are all we possess in most cases. A few other cones in the present collection were bought by Sir Robert Mond at Armant[3], but it is clear that these also were Theban, and their sources can in some instances be identified.

The smaller cones are solid and hand-modelled, often crudely. Some large ones, however, where broken, are seen to be hollow with spiral internal rilling, which suggests that they were coil-built (nos. 138, 143). Generally the name-stamps are in raised relief, no. 140 in sunk relief being a rare exception. The fact that the same stamps occur also on bricks of various shapes has been explained as a device for continuing rows round corners in the superstructure.[4] Stamps containing only the name and titles of the owner, sometimes together with those of parents and/or wife, form the largest category, about 64% of the present collection. The next largest group, about 30%, introduces the owner with the words 'One revered by Osiris.' Examples of both categories in which the owner is 'justified with the great god' or 'justified with Osiris' tend to be of early Dynasty XVIII. A few end, as in some stela inscriptions, with dedications by sons. Other miscellaneous examples include a $htp-di-nsw$ prayer (no. 153) and formulae relating to the solar cult (nos. 31, 128).

Cones may be assigned to known tombs with varying degrees of certainty. While the evidence of name and title alone would hardly be conclusive, some titles are senior enough to limit the field considerably. Identification is more secure where secondary (familiar) names also occur together with the names of parents, wife and offspring, and is strengthened where cones are found in large numbers on or near the site of a tomb. (Isolated finds may, as Gauthier noted[5], occur at long distances from their source.) In case the fact that over 70% of the cones cannot be so attributed should encourage speculation that the tombs might yet be discovered, it should be noted that re-use or usurpation in ancient times was not uncommon.

The arrangement followed in this catalogue is by owners' names in alphabetical order. This has the virtue of putting cones of the same owner together instead of classifying them by the number of lines or columns of text. For ease of reference the Davies-Macadam number is placed first in each bibliography, and a concordance of these numbers, so far as they occur in the present collection, is included at the end. Personal titles, not indexed here, are covered in Davies-Macadam, to which this volume may serve as a supplement. The bibliographies are selective, publications of some parallel examples being excluded where they would add nothing of significance. On the other hand some brief mentions are cited where they offer suggestions about dating or attribution. Dimensions of the stamps are as in the full-scale drawings of Davies, but the lengths are given of complete cones. Only in rare cases has redrawing been necessary.

1. See Eggebrecht A. 'Grabkegel' in Helck et al. *Lexikon der Ägyptologie*; Davies & Macadam, *Corpus . . . Funerary Cones.*
2. Petrie, *Season in Egypt,* 23 ff., pls. 21-23.
3. Mond & Myers, *Temples of Armant,* 101.
4. Borchardt, Königsberger & Ricke in *ZÄS* 70 (1934), 25 ff.
5. Gauthier H. in *BIFAO* 6 (1908), 122 f.

1. AHMOSE

4 cones, stamps only (UC 37573-6).
Attributed to tomb 224, Sheikh Abd el-Qurna.
Dynasty XVIII, temp. Tuthmosis III/Hatshepsut.

4 columns with dividers: 'Overseer of the royal harem, *T*ꜥꜣ-*ms*, tutor (lit. father-nurse), *T*ꜥꜣ-*ms*, chamberlain, *T*ꜥꜣ-*ms*, justified, overseer of cattle, *T*ꜥꜣ-*ms*.'

Bibliography: cf. Davies & Macadam, *Corpus*, no. 94; Daressy, *Recueil*, no. 19; Petrie, *Season*, pl. 22(23); Helck, *Urk.* IV, 1433; Reiser, *Kgl. Harim*, 73; Porter & Moss, *Top. Bibl.* I², 325.

2. AHMOSE

1 cone, stamp only (UC 37588).
Other examples found at Dra Abu el-Naga.[1] Tomb unidentified.
Dynasty XVIII.

4 columns with dividers: 'Chief servant, *T*ꜥꜣ-*ms* (f.), born of the chief servant, *T*ꜥꜣ-*ḥtp* (f.), justified.'

Bibliography: cf. Davies & Macadam, *Corpus,* no. 112; Daressy, *Recueil,* no. 20; Petrie, *Season,* pl. 22(27); Northampton etc. *Theban Necropolis*, pl. 24(21).

Note: 1. Chassinat in *BIFAO* 7 (1910), 159(12).

3. AHMOSE

1 cone, stamp only (UC 37770).
Probably from the same tomb as the previous item.
Dynasty XVIII.

3 columns without dividers: 'Chief servant, supervisor of court women, *T*ꜥꜣ-*ms* (f.), justified.'

Bibliography: cf. Davies & Macadam, *Corpus*, no. 360; Daressy, *Recueil*, no. 66; Petrie, *Season,* pl. 22(54); Northampton etc. *Theban Necropolis*, pl. 24(20).

4. AKHEPERKA

1 cone, stamp only, much abraded (UC 37584).
Duplicate found in the funerary temple of Tuthmosis III at Sheikh Abd el-Qurna.[1] Tomb unidentified.
Early Dynasty XVIII.

4 columns with dividers: 'The Osiris, weapon-bearer of Akheperkare (Tuthmosis I), ⸢*ꜣ-ḫpr-kꜣ*⸣ , justified with the great god.'

Bibliography: cf. Davies & Macadam, *Corpus,* no. 103; Daressy, *Recueil,* no. 36; Petrie,

Season, pl. 21(14); Legrain, *Répertoire,* 112(202).

Note: 1. Weigall in *Ann. Serv.* 7 (1906), 132.

5. AKHEPERKARESONB

1 cone, stamp only (UC 37946).
From West Thebes. Tomb unidentified.
Dynasty XVIII.

3 lines with dividers: '*Wꜥb*-priest of Amun of the first phyle, master of the secrets, ⸢*ꜣ-ḫpr-kꜣ-Rꜥ-snb,* son of *Pꜣ-sꜣ-nsw.*'

Bibliography: cf. Davies & Macadam, *Corpus,* no. 523; Daressy, *Recueil,* no. 184; Petrie, *Season,* pl. 23(82).

6. AMENEMHAB

6 cones, stamps only (UC 37684-9).
Probably from tomb 85, Sheikh Abd el-Qurna. Other examples found in the courtyard of unrelated tomb 89[1] and at Dra Abu el-Naga.[2]
Dynasty XVIII.

2 columns with dividers: 'Lieutenant-commander of the army, *'Imn-m-ḥb.*'

Bibliography: cf. Davies & Macadam, *Corpus,* no. 270; Daressy, *Recueil,* no. 143; Petrie, *Season,* pl. 22(47); Hayes, *Scepter* II, 129; Heyler in *Kêmi* 15 (1959), 89; Porter & Moss, *Top. Bibl.* I². 170 ff.

Notes: 1. Mond in *Ann. Serv.* 6 (1905), 95. 2. Heyler, ibid. 87, n.2 (Strasbourg 386).

7.   AMENEMHAB

1 brick, 16.8 x 7.7 x 3.5 cm. with 2 identical stamps on one face (UC 37992).[1]
From West Thebes, tomb unidentified. Formerly in the Černý Collection.
Dynasty XVIII, temp. Amenophis I.

3 columns with dividers: '$W^c b$-priest of the west side of Amun, '*Imn-m-ḥb.* Son of Re,
Djeserkare (Amenophis I), given life.'

Bibliography: cf. Davies & Macadam, *Corpus,* no. 204; Kees, *Priestertum,* Nachträge,
8 (S.21/22); Hayes, *Scepter* II, 59.

Note: 1. The smooth finish on all sides and the unusual regularity of form raise doubts
about the antiquity of this item, although the matrix of the stamp seems authentic.

8.   AMENEMHAB
Plate 25

1 cone, stamp only (UC 37962).
Perhaps from tomb A.8, Dra Abu el-Naga.[1]
Dynasty XVIII/XIX.

3 lines with dividers: 'True king's scribe[2], whom he loves, overseer of granaries of Amun,
mayor, '*Imn-m-ḥb*, nobleman of the city, /son of/ the dignitary, *Mḥ*, justified.'

Bibliography: cf. Davies & Macadam, *Corpus,* no. 554; Porter & Moss, *Top. Bibl.* I[2], 449 f.

Notes: 1. The occupant, Amenemhab, had a father also called *Mḥ* and similar titles.
2. The full title, *sš- nsw mʒ*^{c}, damaged in Davies' copy, is preserved in the present example
together with further signs of affiliation.

9.   AMENEMHET

1 cone, stamp only (UC 37551).
Attributed to tomb 97, Sheikh Abd el-Qurna.[1]
Dynasty XVIII, temp. Amenophis II(?).

4 columns with dividers in square frame: 'One revered by Osiris, hereditary noble, nomarch,
seal-bearer of the king of Lower Egypt, sole companion, attendant of the lord of the Two
Lands, high-priest of Amun, '*Imn-m-ḥʒt.*'

Bibliography: cf. Davies & Macadam, *Corpus,* no. 43; Daressy, *Recueil,* no. 282; Petrie, *Season,* pl. 23(101); Helck, *Urk.* IV, 1413; Kees, *Priestertum,* Nachträge, 8 (S. 17); Lefebvre, *Histoire des grands prêtres,* 238; Hayes, *Scepter* II, 147; Porter & Moss, *Top. Bibl.* I², 203 f.

Note: 1. Davies, *Tomb of Amenemhet, 2.* n.2 observes that cones of this type were found also in the shaft of tomb 82.

10. AMENEMHET

1 cone, stamp only, left side lost (UC 37587).
Attributed to tomb A. 1, Dra Abu el-Naga.[1] Many examples found in the same area.[2]
Dynasty XVIII.

4 columns with dividers: '*K3*-priest, *'Imn-m-ḥ3 t,* his wife, mistress of the house, *S3t-'Imn,* justified with the great god.'

Bibliography: cf. Davies & Macadam, *Corpus,* no. 110; Daressy, *Recueil,* no. 46; Petrie, *Season,* pl. 21(12).

Notes: 1. Porter & Moss, *Top. Bibl.* I², 447. 2. Gauthier in *BIFAO* 6 (1908), 125 f.

11. AMENEMHET

3 cones, stamps only (UC 37772-4).
Attributed to tomb 123, Sheikh Abd el-Qurna. Example found in courtyard.[1]
Dynasty XVIII, temp. Tuthmosis III.

2 lines without dividers: 'Accountant of grain of Upper and Lower Egypt, *'Imn-m-ḥ3t.*'

Bibliography: cf. Davies & Macadam, *Corpus,* no. 368; Daressy, *Recueil,* no. 249; Petrie, *Season,* pl. 22(67); Mond & Emery in *Liv. Ann.* 14 (1927), 17, fig. 3; Botti, *Antichita Cortona,* no. 246, tav. b; Sethe, *Urk.* IV, 1025 f.(e); Porter & Moss, *Top. Bibl.* I², 236 f.

Note: 1. Mond in *Ann. Serv.* 6 (1905), 94(249), 96.

12. AMENEMHET

1 cone, stamp only, damaged (UC 37819).
From West Thebes. Tomb unidentified.
New Kingdom.

4 lines with dividers: 'One revered by Osiris, w^{c}b-priest of Amun, *'Imn-mḥ3t*, justified.'

Bibliography: cf. Davies & Macadam, *Corpus*, no. 414; Daressy, *Recueil*, no. 204; Petrie, *Season*, pl. 23(72).

13. AMENEMHET

2 cones, stamps only (UC 37960-1).
From West Thebes. Tomb unidentified.
New Kingdom.

3 lines without dividers: 'King's scribe, overseer of the treasury, *'Imn-m-ḥ3t*, justified.'

Bibliography; cf. Davies & Macadam, *Corpus*, no. 552; Daressy, *Recueil*, no. 248;
Petrie, *Season*, pl. 22(65); Helck, *Verwaltung*, 522.

14. AMENEMOPET

1 cone, stamp only (UC 37565).
Attributed to tomb 297, Asasif.
Early Dynasty XVIII.

4 columns with dividers: 'One revered by Osiris, accountant of grain of Amun, overseer of fields, *'Imn-m-ipt* called *Ṯ3-nfr*.'

Bibliography: cf. Davies & Macadam, *Corpus*, no. 73; Daressy, *Recueil*, no. 45; Carter in *Ann. Serv.* 4 (1903), 177 f., fig. B; *Aeg. Inschr. Berlin* II, 300 (1028 etc.); Helck, *Materialien*, 35; Porter & Moss, *Top. Bibl.* I^2, 379.

15. AMENEMOPET

3 cones, stamps only (UC 37681-3).
Attributed to tomb 29, Sheikh Abd el-Qurna.
Dynasty XVIII, temp. Amenophis II.

2 columns without dividers: 'Overseer of the city, vizier, *'Imn-m-ipt*.'

Bibliography: cf. Davies & Macadam, *Corpus*, no. 265; Daressy, *Recueil*, no. 130; Petrie, *Season*, pl. 22(60); Helck, *Verwaltung*, 439; Porter & Moss, *Top. Bibl.* I^2, 45 f.

16. AMENEMOPET

2 cones (UC 37737-8), 1 complete, length 22 cm.
Other examples found at Dra Abu el-Naga.[1] Tomb unidentified.
New Kingdom.

2 columns with dividers: 'Chief bowman, overseer of hunters, *'Imn-m-ỉpt.'*

Bibliography: cf. Davies & Macadam, *Corpus,* no. 304; Daressy, *Recueil,* no. 142; Petrie, *Season,* pl. 22(46); Helck, *Materialien,* 41; id. *Militärführer,* 27; Heyler in *Kêmi* 15 (1959), 89.

Note: 1. Heyler, ibid. 87, n.2 (Strasbourg 373, 384, 399).

17. AMENEMOPET

1 cone, stamp only (UC 37764).
From West Thebes. Tomb unidentified.[1]
Dynasty XVIII/XIX.

2 columns without dividers: 'Conductor of festivals of Amun, chief steward, *'Imn-m-ỉpt.'*

Bibliography: cf. Davies & Macadam, *Corpus,* no. 321; Kees, *Priestertum,* Nachträge, 28 (S.323).

Note: 1. Tomb 41, Sheikh Abd el-Qurna, belonged to a 'chief steward of Amun in the Southern City', perhaps the same man; see Porter & Moss, *Top. Bibl.* I², 78 ff.

18. AMENHOTEP

1 cone, stamp only, damaged (UC 37556).
Other examples found at Dra Abu el-Naga.[1] Tomb unidentified.
New Kingdom.

4 columns with dividers: 'One revered by Osiris, $w^c b$-priest, singer of Amun of the third[2] phyle, scribe of the district[3] in the southern city (i.e. Thebes), *'Imn-ḥtp.'*

Bibliography: cf. Davies & Macadam, *Corpus,* no. 46; Daressy, *Recueil,* no. 50; Petrie, *Season,* pl. 21(13).

Notes: 1. Gauthier in *BIFAO* 6 (1908), 126. 2,3. Restored after Gauthier. See also Helck in *OLZ* 1959, 371.

19. AMENHOTEP

1 cone, stamp only (UC 37566).
From West Thebes. Tomb unidentified.
Dynasty XVIII.

4 columns with dividers: 'One revered by Osiris, secretary of the high-priest, *'Imn-ḥtp* called *Smn*, son of the scribe, *'Imn-ḥtp, justified.*'

Bibliography: cf. Davies & Macadam, *Corpus,* no. 74; Daressy, *Recueil,* no. 49; Helck, *Materialien,* 52.

20. AMENHOTEP

1 cone, stamp only (UC 37589).
From West Thebes. Tomb unidentified.
New Kingdom.

4 columns with dividers: 'Scribe, steward of the high-priest of Amen-Re, *'Imn-ḥtp,* justified.'

Bibliography: cf. Davies & Macadam, *Corpus* no. 123; Daressy, *Recueil,* no. 22; Petrie, *Season,* pl. 22(20); *Aeg. Inschr. Berlin* II, 300(1023); Helck, *Materialien,* 52.

21. AMENHOTEP

3 cones, stamps only (UC 30182, 37590-1).
From West Thebes. Tomb unidentified.
New Kingdom.

4 columns with dividers: 'Scribe, overseer of granaries of the god's-wife, *'Imn-ḥtp,* justified. Mistress of the house, *Rwiw,* justified. Begotten[1] by the overseer of granaries, *K3k3,* born of the mistress of the house, *Mḥ,* justified.'

Bibliography: cf. Davies & Macadam, *Corpus,* no. 124; Daressy, *Recueil,* no. 21; Petrie, *Season,* pl. 22(21); Helck, *Materialien,* 123.

Note: 1. Presumably referring to the former.

22. AMENHOTEP

1 cone, stamp only (UC 37604).
Other examples found at Dra Abu el-Naga.[1] Tomb unidentified.
New Kingdom.

3 columns without dividers: 'One revered by Osiris, the acolyte of Amun of the 4th phyle, *'Imn-ḥtp,* justified.'

Bibliography: cf. Davies & Macadam, *Corpus,* no. 151; Daressy, *Recueil,* no. 100; Helck, *Materialien,* 51; Kees, *Priestertum,* Nachträge, 26(S.301).

Note: 1. Gauthier in *BIFAO* 6 (1908), 126 f.

23. AMENHOTEP

1 cone, stamp only (UC 37616).
From West Thebes. Tomb unidentified.
New Kingdom.

3 columns with dividers: 'One revered by Osiris, the fourth prophet of Amun, *'Imn-ḥtp,* justified.'

Bibliography: cf. Davies & Macadam, *Corpus,* no. 162; Daressy, *Recueil,* no. 109; Petrie, *Season,* pl. 22(32).

24. AMENHOTEP

1 cone, stamp only (UC 37617).
From West Thebes. Tomb unidentified.
New Kingdom.

3 columns with dividers: 'One revered by Osiris, the chief coppersmith, *'Imn·ḥtp,* justified. His sister, mistress of the house, *'Irty,* justified.'

Bibliography: cf. Davies & Macadam, *Corpus,* no. 164; Daressy, *Recueil,* no. 108; Petrie, *Season,* pl. 22(31); *Aeg. Inschr. Berlin* II, 300(7644).

25. AMENHOTEP

1 cone, point missing (UC 37642).
From West Thebes. Tomb unidentified.
Dynasty XVIII.

3 columns without dividers: 'Overseer of builders of Amun, *'Imn-ḥtp,* justified, son of the overseer of builders, *Snn3.*'

Bibliography: cf. Davies & Macadam, *Corpus,* no. 185; Northampton etc. *Theban Necropolis,* pl. 24(30); Helck, *Materialien,* 45; Hayes, *Scepter* II, 225.

26. AMENHOTEP

1 cone, stamp only (UC 37644).
Other examples found at Dra Abu el-Naga.[1] Tomb unidentified.
New Kingdom.

3 columns without dividers in square frame: 'Overseer of craftsmen of Min and Isis, *'Imn-ḥtp,* justified. His sister, mistress of the house, *Ḳdt-mrt.*'

Bibliography: cf. Davies & Macadam, *Corpus,* no. 192; Daressy, *Recueil,* no. 284; Petrie, *Season,* pl. 23(102); *Aeg. Inschr. Berlin* II, 292 (8769 ff.), Helck, *Materialien,* 172.

Note: 1. Gauthier in *BIFAO* 6 (1908), 129 f.

27. AMENHOTEP

2 cones, points missing (UC 37649-50).
Other examples found at Dra Abu el-Naga.[1] Tomb unidentified.
Dynasty XVIII.

3 columns with dividers: 'The Osiris, steward of Amun, high-priest of (Queen) Nefertari[2], steward, *'Imn-ḥtp,* justified.'

Bibliography: cf. Davies & Macadam, *Corpus,* no. 210; Helck, *Materialien,* 29, 87.

Notes: 1. Gauthier in *BIFAO* 6 (1908), 130 f. 2. The mother of Amenophis I.

28. AMENHOTEP

2 cones, stamps only (UC 37656-7).
From West Thebes. Tomb unidentified.
New Kingdom.

3 columns with dividers: 'The Osiris, accountant of cattle of Amun, *'Imn-ḥtp*, justified. His wife, mistress of the house, *Sзt-'Imn.*'

Bibliography: cf. Davies & Macadam, *Corpus*, no. 217; Daressy, *Recueil*, no. 107; Petrie, *Season*, pl. 22(37); Northampton etc. *Theban Necropolis*, pl. 25(41); Helck, *Materialien*, 32.

29. AMENHOTEP

1 cone, stamp only, damaged (UC 37732).
From West Thebes. Tomb unidentified.
New Kingdom.

2 columns with dividers: 'The Osiris, chief corn-measurer of Amun, *'Imn-ḥtp.*'

Bibliography: cf. Davies & Macadam, *Corpus*, no. 288; Daressy, *Recueil*, no. 152; Helck, *Materialien*, 35.

30. AMENHOTEP

1 cone, stamp only (UC 37769).
From West Thebes. Tomb unidentified.
New Kingdom.

1 column and 3 lines without dividers: 'One revered by Osiris, scribe of all the craftsmen of Amun, *'Imn-ḥtp.*'

Bibliography: cf. Davies & Macadam, *Corpus*, no. 354; Daressy, *Recueil*, no. 101; Helck, *Materialien*, 46.

31. AMENHOTEP

1 cone, stamp only, damaged (UC 37976).
From West Thebes. Tomb unidentified.
Dynasty XVIII.

3 columns and 1 line with dividers and kneeling figure: 'Adoration of Re, when he goes to rest in life, by the scribe of the offering-table of Amun, *'Imn-ḥtp*, justified.'

Bibliography: cf. Davies & Macadam, *Corpus*, no. 597; Daressy, *Recueil*, no. 266; Botti, *Antichita Cortona*, no. 247.

32. AMENNAKHT

2 cones, stamps only (UC 37567-8).
From West Thebes. Tomb unidentified.
New Kingdom.

4 columns with dividers: 'One revered by Osiris, the king's chief, eldest *[*son*]*, *'Imn-nḫt*[1], justified with Amun. His sister, mistress of the house, *Mwt-nfrt.*'

Bibliography: cf. Davies & Macadam, *Corpus,* no. 76; Daressy, *Recueil,* no. 48 (miscopied); Petrie, *Season,* pl. 21(9).

Note: 1. Helck in *OLZ* 1959, 371, amends the man's title to *[s3-] nsw tpy n ḥ3t 'Imn,* leaving *Nḫt* as the name.

33. AMENWERKEN

1 cone, stamp only, damaged (UC 37771).
From West Thebes. Tomb unidentified.
Dynasty XVIII.

3 columns without dividers: 'Scribe, *'Imn-wr-ḳn,* repeating life, justified, son of the scribe, *Nfr-m-ḥb.*'

Bibliography: cf. Davies & Macadam, *Corpus,* no. 363; Daressy, *Recueil,* no. 67; Petrie, *Season,* pl. 22(55).

34. ANEN

4 cones, stamps only (UC 37634-7).
Other examples found at Dra Abu el-Naga.[1] Tomb unidentified.
New Kingdom.

3 columns with dividers: 'One revered by Osiris, scribe, *ʿnn.*'

Bibliography: cf. Davies & Macadam, *Corpus,* no. 172; Daressy, *Recueil,* no. 114; Petrie, *Season,* pl. 22(34).

Note: 1. Gauthier in *BIFAO* 6 (1908), 129.

35. ANTEF

2 cones, stamps only (UC 37601-2).
Attributed to tomb 155, Dra Abu el-Naga, where other examples also found.[1]
Dynasty XVIII, temp. Hatshepsut/Tuthmosis III.

3 columns without dividers: 'One revered by Anubis who is upon his mountain, king's herald, *'In-itf,* justified.'

Bibliography: cf. Davies & Macadam, *Corpus,* no. 139; Daressy, *Recueil,* no. 110; James, *Corpus Brooklyn,* no. 186; Sethe, *Urk.* IV, 975 (281); Helck, *Verwaltung,* 495; Porter & Moss, *Top. Bibl.* I², 263 ff.

Note: Gauthier in *BIFAO* 6 (1908), 127 f.

36. BASA

2 cones, stamps only (UC 37571-2).
From West Thebes. Tomb unidentified.[1]
Dynasty XXVI.

4 columns with dividers in square frame: 'Hereditary noble, nomarch, prophet of Amen-Re, king of the gods, overseer of prophets of the gods of Upper Egypt, overseer of the entire Southern City, chief steward of the divine votaress, *B3s3,* justified, son of the beloved of the god, *P3-di-B3stt,* justified.'

Bibliography: cf. Davies & Macadam, *Corpus,* no. 92; Daressy, *Recueil,* no. 281.

Note: 1. The owner of tomb 389 had a father of different name.

37. BENGY

1 cone, upper half of stamp only. Sides of cone slightly flattened (UC 37677).
Other examples found at Dra Abu el-Naga.[1] Tomb unidentified.
Dynasty XVIII.

2 columns without dividers: 'Steward of *Hnwt-m-pt* (?)[2], *Bngy,* justified.'

Bibliography: cf. Davies & Macadam, *Corpus,* no. 260; Northampton etc. *Theban Necropolis,* pl. 25(45); Heyler in *Kêmi* 15 (1959), 89; Helck, *Materialien,* 212.

Notes: 1. Heyler, ibid. 87, n.2 (Strasbourg 375, 400, 407). 2. Such a name is attested in Ranke, *Personennamen* I, 243(7), but would be odd in this context. Helck in *OLZ* 1959, 371 f. suggests amendment to *ḥnwt-tȝwy*, 'mistress of the Two Lands.' The present impression, being damaged, does not allow Davies' copy to be verified, and Northampton treats the words *m pt* as a restoration. Another cone of *Bȝgy* (Davies & Macadam no. 527 = Daressy no. 237), however, describes him as major-domo of the princess of Naharin, a person to whom the disputed name (or title?) might conceivably have applied.

38. DEDU

1 cone, stamp only (UC 37512).
Attributed to tomb 200, Khokha.[1]
Dynasty XVIII, temp. Tuthmosis III - Amenophis II.

5 columns with dividers: 'King's messenger in all foreign lands, so great is his excellence in the opinion of those who awarded him the gold of favour for valour on many occasions. Chief of the Medjay, *Ddw*, justified.'

Bibliography: cf. Davies & Macadam, *Corpus,* no. 4; Daressy, *Recueil,* no. 13; Petrie, *Season,* pl. 21(2); Sethe, *Urk.* IV, 995(d); Hayes, *Scepter* II, 129; Helck, *Materialien,* 966; Porter & Moss, *Top. Bibl.* I², 303 f.

Note: 1. See also the following two items.

39. DEDU

1 cone, stamp only (UC 37525).
Attributed to tomb 200, Khokha.
Dynasty XVIII, temp. Tuthmosis III - Amenophis II.

5 columns with dividers: 'Captain of the ship 'Beloved-of-Amun', standard-bearer of the troops of his Majesty, overseer of the hill-country on the west of Thebes, chief of the Medjay, *Dd w, justified with the great god, lord of the necropolis.'*

Bibliography: cf. Davies & Macadam, *Corpus,* no. 22; Daressy, *Recueil,* no. 4; Petrie, *Season,* pl. 22(26); Sethe, *Urk.* IV, 996(f); Hayes, *Scepter* II, 129; Schulman, *Military Rank,* 137 (323e).

40. DEDU

1 cone, stamp only (UC 37526).
Attributed to tomb 200, Khokha.[1]
Dynasty XVIII, temp. Tuthmosis III - Amenophis II.

5 columns with dividers: 'Trusty confidant of the lord of the Two Lands, valiant warrior of the infantry, who pleases the hearts of the entire land, so greatly is he loved, chief (of the Medjay)[2], *Ddw,* justified.'

Bibliography: cf. Davies & Macadam, *Corpus,* no. 24; Daressy, *Recueil,* no. 30; Petrie, *Season,* pl. 22(25); Sethe, *Urk.* IV, 995(e); David, *The Macclesfield Collection,* 54(27), pl. E.27; Helck in *OLZ* 1959, 370; Hayes, *Scepter* II, 129.

Notes: 1. The Macclesfield example was found at Dra Abu el-Naga. 2. Cf. the previous item. See also Helck, ibid.

41. DENREG

4 cones, including 1 complete, length 24.4 cm. (UC 37552-5).
Other examples found at Qurnet Murai.[1] Tomb unidentified.
New Kingdom.

4 columns with dividers: 'One revered by Osiris, chief *wᶜb*-priest, *Dnrg, justified.'*

Bibliography: cf. Davies & Macadam, *Corpus,* no. 45; Daressy, *Recueil,* no. 60; Petrie, *Season,* pl. 21(5); *Aeg. Inschr. Berlin* II, 300 (19595).

Note: 1. Gauthier in *BIFAO* 16 (1919), 175 f.

42. DJEDHIR

2 cones, stamps only, damaged (UC 37775-6).
From West Thebes. Tomb unidentified.
Dynasty XXII(?).

6 lines with dividers: '*Dd-ḥr,* justified(?)[1], son of *ᶜnh-ḥr,* son of the hereditary noble, nomarch, great chief of the Meshwesh, nomarch, overseer of prophets of the ram, lord of Mendes, *Dd-ḥr,* his (i.e. the owner of the cone's) mother being the mistress of the house, *Šp-n-spdt,* justified.'

Bibliography: cf. Davies & Macadam, *Corpus,* no. 378; Daressy, *Recueil,* no. 156; Petrie, *Season,* pl. 23(99); Kees, *Priestertum,* 202, n. 4; Schulman, *Military Rank,* 139 (340).

Note: 1. Daressy omits this group, putting the seated man determinative at the end of the line. The examples in U.C. are damaged at that point.

43. DJEHUTIEMHAB

1 cone, stamp only (UC 37564).
Other examples found at Dra Abu el-Naga.[1] Tomb unidentified.
Dynasty XVIII.

4 columns with dividers: 'One revered by Osiris, scribe of the southern city, *Ḏḥwty-m-ḥb* called *Wn-ỉr-sw,* justified.'

Bibliography: cf. Davies & Macadam, *Corpus,* no. 64; Daressy, *Recueil,* no. 62; Petrie, *Season,* pl. 21(7); Ranke, *Personennamen* I, 78(17).

Note: 1. Gauthier in *BIFAO* 6 (1908), 126.

44. DJEHUTINEFER

2 cones, stamps only (UC 30174, 37643).
From West Thebes. Tomb unidentified.
New Kingdom.

3 columns without dividers: 'Steward of the god's-wife, *Ḏḥwty-nfr,* justified.'

Bibliography: cf. Davies & Macadam, *Corpus,* no. 189; Daressy, *Recueil,* no. 140; Petrie, *Season,* pl. 22(58); Helck, *Materialien,* 123.

45. DJEHUTINEFER

2 cones, stamps only (UC 37800-1).
Attributable to tomb A.6, Dra Abu el-Naga.[1]
Dynasty XX.

5 lines with dividers: 'The Osiris, accountant of cattle and game-birds of Amun, *Ḏḥwty-nfr* called *Snw* (or *Sšw*), justified, son of the scribe, *Msw,* justified.'

Bibliography: cf. Davies & Macadam, *Corpus,* no. 397; Daressy, *Recueil,* no. 165; Petrie, *Season,* pl. 23(95); Northampton etc. *Theban Necropolis,* pl. 24(27); Helck, *Materialien,* 32; Ranke, *Personennamen* I, 297(6).

Note: 1. Porter & Moss, *Top. Bibl.* I², 449; Gauthier in *BIFAO* 6 (1908), 124 f. (on other cones of the same man = Davies' nos. 14 and 396).

46. DJEHUTMOSE

39 cones, including 25 complete, max. length 23.2 cm., all double-stamped (UC 37690-37728).
2 bricks, wedge-shaped: (a) 19.0 x 12.2 x 4.5 cm. with 4 stamps on one edge and 2 on end (UC 37729); (b) 17.5 x 11.6 x 6.0 cm. with 3 stamps on one edge and 2 on end (UC 37730).
Other examples of cones found at Dra Abu el-Naga.[1] Tomb unidentified.
New Kingdom.

2 columns without dividers in rectangular frame: 'Chief $w^c b$-priest of Amun, *Ḏḥwty-ms.*'

Bibliography: cf. Davies & Macadam, *Corpus,* no. 271; Daressy, *Recueil,* no. 149.

Note: 1. Gauthier in *BIFAO* 6 (1908), 129.

47. DJEHUTY

1 cone, stamp only (UC 37676).
Attributed to tomb 11, Dra Abu el-Naga.[1]
Dynasty XVIII, temp. Hatshepsut - Tuthmosis III.

2 columns with dividers: 'Overseer of cattle of Amun, nomarch, *Ḏḥwty.*'

Bibliography: cf. Davies & Macadam, *Corpus,* no. 257; Daressy, *Recueil,* no. 147; Petrie, *Season,* pl. 22(44); Northampton etc. *Theban Necropolis,* pl. 24(23); Heyler in *Kêmi* 15 (1959), 89; Porter & Moss, *Top. Bibl.* I², 21 ff.

Note: 1. Heyler, ibid. 86, n. 5. See also the following item.

48. DJEHUTY

2 cones, stamps only (UC 37678-9).
Attributed to tomb 11, Dra Abu el-Naga.
Dynasty XVIII, temp. Hatshepsut - Tuthmosis III.

2 columns with dividers: 'Overseer of the treasury, overseer of works, *Ḏḥwty*, justified.'

Bibliography: cf. Davies & Macadam, *Corpus,* no. 263; Daressy, *Recueil,* no. 148;
Petrie, *Season,* pl. 22(43); Northampton etc. *Theban Necropolis,* pl. 24(16); Helck,
Verwaltung, 508.

49. DJESERKA

2 cones, stamps only (UC 37733-4).
From West Thebes. Tomb unidentified.
Dynasty XVIII(?).

2 columns with dividers in square frame: 'Osiris, great god, lord of heaven and earth. Chief
wˁb-priest, *Ḏsr-kȝ*.'

Bibliography: cf. Davies & Macadam, *Corpus,* no. 294; Daressy, *Recueil,* no. 288; Petrie,
Season, pl. 23(104).

50. ES

2 cones, stamps only (UC 37513, 37981).
From West Thebes.[1] Tomb unidentified.
Dynasty XVIII.

5 columns with dividers: 'One revered by Osiris, steward of Amun in the oasis, overseer of
granaries of Amun, nomarch of the northern oasis, scribe *S*, justified with the great god,
lord of eternity.[1]

Bibliography: cf. Davies & Macadam, *Corpus,* no. 5; Helck, *Materialien,* 30, 33, 43.

Note: 1. A duplicate of this cone was amongst others bought at Sheikh Abd el-Qurna and
Asasif; see Heyler in *Kêmi* 15 (1959), 87, n. 2 (Strasbourg no. 999).

51. HATMESHA

11 cones, points missing, max. length 8.2 cm. (UC 37739-49).
From West Thebes. Tomb unidentified.
New Kingdom.

2 columns without dividers: 'Chief bowman, $H3t$-$m\check{s}^{\varsigma}$.'

Bibliography: cf. Davies & Macadam, *Corpus,* no. 306; Daressy, *Recueil,* no. 252; Petrie, *Season,* pl. 22(59).

52. HEBY

3 cones, stamps only (UC 37522-4).
Other examples found at Dra Abu el-Naga.[1] Tomb unidentified.
Dynasty XVIII, temp. Amenophis III.

5 columns with dividers: 'One revered by Osiris, accountant of cattle of Amun throughout the nomes of Upper and Lower Egypt, *Hby,* justified, son of the accountant of cattle of Amun, *Sn-ms,* justified, born of the mistress of the house, *Rwi.*'

Bibliography: cf. Davies & Macadam, *Corpus,* no. 15; Daressy, *Recueil,* no. 10; Petrie, *Season,* pl. 21(1); Northampton etc. *Theban Necropolis,* pl. 25(32); *Aeg. Inschr. Berlin* II, 291 (1615); Helck, *Urk.* IV, 1792; id. *Materialien,* 32.

Note: 1. Gauthier in *BIFAO* 6 (1908), 124 f.

53. HEBY

1 cone, stamp only (UC 37640).
Other examples found in vicinity of unrelated tomb 23, Sheikh Abd el-Qurna.[1] Source unidentified.
New Kingdom.

3 columns with dividers: 'One revered by Osiris, servant of Amun[2], *Hby,* justified.'

Bibliography: cf. Davies & Macadam, *Corpus,* no. 180; Daressy, *Recueil,* no. 118; Petrie, *Season,* pl. 22(35); Helck, *Materialien,* 49; Schulman, *Military Rank,* 162(475).

Notes: 1. Collins L. in *JEA* 62 (1976), 34. 2. Misread by Schulman as 'valiant one of the army' from Petrie's damaged version.

54. HEPU

1 cone, stamp only, damaged (UC 37973).
Attributed to tomb 66, Sheikh Abd el-Qurna.
Dynasty XVIII, temp. Tuthmosis IV.

1 column before standing figure: 'Overseer of the city, vizier, *Ḥpw,* justified.'

Bibliography: cf. Davies & Macadam, *Corpus,* no. 583; Daressy, *Recueil,* no. 270; Petrie, *Season,* pl. 22(62); Helck, *Verwaltung,* 440; Porter & Moss, *Top. Bibl.* I^2, 132 f.

55. HIRYTEPHUTAMUN

1 cone, stamp only (UC 37957).
From West Thebes. Tomb unidentified.
New Kingdom.

3 lines with dividers: 'Scribe, *Ḥry-tp-ḥwt-'Imn,* justified.'

Bibliography: cf. Davies & Macadam, *Corpus,* no. 547; Daressy, *Recueil,* no. 229(?), probably miscopied from a poor original.

56. HOR

19 cones, points missing, max. length 22 cm. (UC 37527-45).
From West Thebes. Tomb unidentified.
Dynasty XXII.

5 columns without dividers: 'Prophet of Monthu, secretary of the palace, *Ḥr,* justified; prophet of Amun, hereditary noble, nomarch, *Ḥr,* justified.' In the middle column is the cartouche of Usermaetre-meriamun Sheshonq (IV).

Bibliography: cf. Davies & Macadam, *Corpus,* no. 26; Daressy, *Recueil,* no. 77; Petrie, *Season,* pl. 22(56); Gauthier, *Livre des rois* III, 370; Kees, *Priestertum,* 310, n.5.

57. IBI

1 cone, stamp only (UC 30181).
Attributed to tomb 36, Asasif, where many examples found.[1]
Dynasty XXVI, temp. Psammetikhos I.

4 lines with dividers: 'Hereditary noble, nomarch, seal-bearer of the king of Lower Egypt, beloved sole companion, king's acquaintance, chief steward of the god's-wife, *'Ib3ỉ*, son of the beloved of the god, *ʿnḫ-Ḥr*, justified.'

Bibliography: cf. Davies & Macadam, *Corpus,* no. 450; Daressy, *Recueil,* no. 177; Petrie, *Season,* pl. 23(93); Porter & Moss, *Top. Bibl.* I², 63 ff.

Note: 1. 'Fouilles de l'Assassif 1970-75' in *Chron. d'Égypte* 50 (1975), 14 ff., particularly 19.

58. INENI

6 cones, stamps only (UC 37847-52).
Attributed to tomb 81, Sheikh Abd el-Qurna.[1]
Dynasty XVIII, temp. Amenophis I - Tuthmosis III.

4 lines without dividers: 'Nomarch, overseer of granaries of Amun, overseer of all seal-bearers in the temple of Amun, scribe, *'Inn,* justified.'

Bibliography: cf. Davies & Macadam, *Corpus,* no. 480; Daressy, *Recueil,* no. 170; Petrie, *Season,* pl. 22(70); Mond & Emery in *Liv. Ann.* 14 (1972), 33, fig. 25; Porter & Moss, *Top. Bibl.* I², 159 ff.

Note: 1. Daressy, loc. cit. ('Champollion no. 5'); Mond in *Ann. Serv.* 6 (1905), 95.

59. INHERTMOSE

2 cones, including 1 complete, length 21.2 cm. (UC 37824-5).
2 bricks, wedge-shaped, fragments only: (a) length 16.0 cm. with 2 stamps on one face (UC 37826); (b) length 15.0 cm. with 2 stamps on one face and another on end (UC 37827). Further examples of cones found at Sheikh Abd el-Qurna.[1] Tomb unidentified.
Dynasty XVIII, temp. Amenophis III.

4 lines with dividers: 'One revered by Osiris, scribe of works of the (funerary) temple of Amenophis III (*ḥwt Nb-m3ʿt-Rʿ*)[2] on the west of Thebes, *'Inḥrt-ms,* justified with the great god.'

Bibliography: cf. Davies & Macadam, *Corpus,* no. 430; Daressy, *Recueil,* no. 206; Petrie, *Season,* pl. 23(84); *Aeg. Inschr. Berlin* II, 299 (8744) etc.); Botti, *Antichita Cortona,* no. 240, tav. a; Helck, *Urk.* IV, 1941; id. *Materialien,* 99; Heyler in *Kêmi* 15 (1959), 91.

Notes: 1. Legrain, *Répertoire*, 147(257); Heyler, ibid. 87, n.2. 2. Otto, *Topographie des thebanischen Gaues*, 67 f., 113.

60. IRINEFERUEF

1 cone, stamp only (UC 37516).
From West Thebes. Tomb unidentified.
Dynasty XVIII.

5 columns with dividers: 'One revered by Osiris, /storekeeper(?)/[1] of Amun, *'Ir-nfrw.f*, justified. His wife, mistress of the house, *3ḥ-Mwt*, justified.'

Bibliography: cf. Davies & Macadam, *Corpus*, n o.7; Helck, *Materialien*, 47; id. in *OLZ* 1959, 370.

Note: 1. Helck in *OLZ* suggests the restoration *iry-'t* on the basis of a statue inscription (Brit. Mus. 29), perhaps of the same man; see Porter & Moss, *Top. Bibl.* I², 789.

61. IY

2 bricks (?), fragments only, each with one stamp (UC 37765-6).
From West Thebes. Tomb unidentified.
New Kingdom.

1 column in oval frame: 'Overseer of weavers, *'Iy*.'

Bibliography: cf. Davies & Macadam, *Corpus*, no. 334; Daressy, *Recueil*, no. 275; Petrie, *Season*, pl. 23(106); Northampton etc. *Theban Necropolis*, pl. 25(40); *Aeg. Inschr. Berlin* II, 292 (1032).

62. KAEMAMUN

1 cone, stamp only (UC 37975).[1]
From West Thebes. Tomb unidentified.[2]
Mid-Dynasty XVIII.

3 columns and 1 line before a kneeling figure, all within a rectangular frame: 'Seal-bearer of the king of Lower Egypt, fourth prophet of Amun, *K3-m-'Imn*, justified. His son, second prophet of Menkheperre (Tuthmosis III), *S-ḳd*.'

Bibliography: cf. Davies & Macadam, *Corpus,* no. 590; Daressy, *Recueil,* no. 294; Helck, *Materialien,* 96; Kees, *Priestertum,* Nachträge, 9 (S.24).

Notes: 1. See also the following two items. 2. For other monuments of this individual see De Buck in *JEOL* 15 (1957-8), 5 f.; James, *Corpus Brooklyn,* no. 210 (= our no.63); Porter & Moss, *Top. Bibl.* I², 627.

63. KAEMAMUN

1 brick, fragment only, with two stamps on one face (UC 37671).
From West Thebes. Tomb unidentified.
Mid-Dynasty XVIII.

3 columns without dividers: 'Seal-bearer of the king of Lower Egypt, fourth prophet of Amun, *K3-m-'Imn,* justified.'

Bibliography: cf. Davies & Macadam, *Corpus,* no. 246; Daressy, *Recueil,* no. 80; Petrie, *Season,* pl. 22(53); *Aeg. Inschr. Berlin* II, 297 (13204); James, loc. cit.; Hayes, *Scepter* II, 118; Droste von & Schlick-Nolte, *CAA: Rhein-Main* I, 1,123 f.

64. KAEMAMUN (AMUNEMKA)

1 cone, stamp only (UC 37659).
From West Thebes. Tomb unidentified.
Mid-Dynasty XVIII.

3 columns with dividers: 'Second prophet of Menkheperre (Tuthmosis III), *'Imn-m-k3* (sic).[1] His wife, musician, *Mryt-R^c.*'

Bibliography: cf. Davies & Macadam, *Corpus,* no. 228; Daressy, *Recueil,* no. 82; Petrie, *Season,* pl. 22(39); Helck, *Materialien,* 95; Kees, *Priestertum,* Nachträge, 9 (S.24); Hayes, *Scepter* II, 118; Droste von & Schlick-Nolte, *CAA: Rhein-Main* I, 1,127 f.

Note: 1. Presumably the same individual as in the previous two items; see D Buck op. cit. James, loc. cit.

65. KANAKHT

3 cones, stamps only (UC 37954-6).
From West Thebes. Tomb unidentified.
New Kingdom.

3 lines with dividers: 'Mayor of Hermonthis, *K3-nḫt.*'

Bibliography: cf. Davies & Macadam, *Corpus,* no. 534; Daressy, *Recueil,* no. 232; Petrie, *Season,* pl. 23(81); Helck, *Materialien,* 160.

66. KHA

2 cones, stamps only, damaged (UC 37618-9).
Other examples found at Dra Abu el-Naga.[1] Tomb unidentified.
New Kingdom.

3 columns with dividers: 'One revered by Osiris, chief retainer of the house, *Ḫꜥ,* justified. His wife, mistress of the house, *Ḥnwt-t3wy.*'

Bibliography: cf. Davies & Macadam, *Corpus,* no. 168; Daressy, *Recueil,* no. 120; Petrie, *Season,* pl. 22(33).

Note: 1. Gauthier in *BIFAO* 6 (1908), 129.

67. KHAUT

8 cones, including 1 complete, length 21 cm. (UC 37831-8).
From West Thebes.[1] Tomb unidentified.
Dynasty XVIII(?)

4 lines with dividers: 'The Osiris, priest-in-front of Amun, deputy in the temple of Amun, *Ḥ3wt,*[2] justified. His sister, whom he loves, the musician of Amun, mistress of the house, *T3-(nt-)Mwt,* justified.'

Bibliography: cf. Davies & Macadam, *Corpus,* no. 465; Daressy, *Recueil,* no. 195; Petrie, *Season,* pl. 23(89); Heyler in *Kêmi* 15 (1959), 91, pl. 14, fig. 7; Helck, *Materialien,* 38.

Notes: 1. A duplicate, Strasbourg 1004, was among cones bought at Sheikh Abd el-Qurna and Asasif; see Heyler, op. cit. 87, n.2. 2. Perhaps the same owner as of the pyramidion Brit. Mus. 707; see Porter & Moss, *Top. Bibl.* I², 836, and Brit. Mus. *Guide (Sculpture),* 155(558).

68. KHAWY

8 cones, points missing, max. length 22.8 cm. (UC 37777-84).
From West Thebes. Tomb unidentified.
New Kingdom.

5 lines with dividers: 'One revered by Osiris, doorkeeper of Amun in the forecourt[1], *Ḫꜣwy*, justified.'

Bibliography: cf. Davies & Macadam, *Corpus*, no. 383; Helck, *Materialien*, 50.

Note: 1. The present examples supply the 'drill' sign, lost in Davies' copy, and confirm the reading *wbꜣ*.

69. KHONS

1 cone, stamp only, right side lost (UC 37680).
From West Thebes. Tomb unidentified.
Dynasty XVIII(?).

2 columns with divider: 'Overseer of the treasury, scribe, *Ḫnsw*,'

Bibliography: cf. Davies & Macadam, *Corpus*, no. 264; Daressy, *Recueil*, no. 146; Petrie, *Season*, pl. 22(45); Helck, *Verwaltung*, 515.

70. MAETY

2 cones, stamps only (UC 37860-1).
Duplicate found at Asasif near unrelated tomb 33[1], another at Sheikh Abd el-Qurna on the mortuary temple site of Tuthmosis III[2]. Source unidentified.
Dynasty XVIII.

3 lines with dividers: 'One revered by Osiris, scribe, *Mꜣꜥty*. Mistress of the house, *Ḥwy*.'

Bibliography: cf. Davies & Macadam, *Corpus*, no. 503; Daressy, *Recueil*, no. 241; Petrie, *Season*, pl. 23(71); *Aeg. Inschr. Berlin* II, 301 (9605).

Notes: 1. Chassinat in *BIFAO* 7 (1910), 161 (19). 2. *Aeg. Inschr. Berlin* II, loc. cit.

71. MAHU

2 cones, stamps only (UC 37651-2).
From West Thebes. Tomb unidentified.
Dynasty XVIII(?).

3 columns with dividers: 'The Osiris, keeper of poultry of Amun, *Mḥ*, justified with the great god.'

Bibliography: cf. **Davies & Macadam**, *Corpus*, no. 212; Helck, *Materialien*, 41.

72. MAHU

1 cone, stamp only (UC 37974).
From West Thebes. Tomb unidentified.
New Kingdom.

Caption before kneeling figure: 'Guardian of the treasury of the king, *Mḥ*.'

Bibliography: cf. **Davies & Macadam**, *Corpus*, no. 587 (with 588); Daressy, *Recueil*, no. 269; Petrie, *Season*, pl. 22(63).

73. MAY

1 cone, stamp only (UC 37550).
From West Thebes. Tomb unidentified.
New Kingdom.

4 columns with dividers: 'One revered by (Osiris)[1], hereditary prince, nomarch, overseer of horn, hoof, feather and scale (i.e. all livestock), overseer of cattle of Amun, *My*, justified.'

Bibliography: cf. **Davies & Macadam**, *Corpus*, no. 41; Daressy, *Recueil*, no. 53; Petrie, *Season*, pl. 21(10); Helck, *Materialien*, 31.

Note: 1. The name of Osiris has been omitted.

74 . MENKHEPER

1 cone, stamp only, right half lost (UC 37648).
Duplicate found at Dra Abu el-Naga.[1] Tomb unidentified.
New Kingdom.

3 columns with dividers: '$W^c b$-priest of Amun of the second phyle, *Mn-ḥpr.* His wife, mistress of the house, *Mwt-nfrt.*'

Bibliography: cf. Davies & Macadam, *Corpus,* no. 206; Heyler in *Kêmi* 15 (1959), 89.

Note: 1. Heyler, ibid. 87, n.2 (Strasbourg 381).

75. MENKHEPERRESONB

6 cones, stamps only (UC 37578-83).
Attributed to tomb 86, Sheikh Abd el-Qurna.[1]
Dynasty XVIII, temp. Tuthmosis III.

4 columns with dividers: 'The Osiris, hereditary noble, nomarch, seal-bearer of the king of Lower Egypt, high-priest of Amun, *Mn-ḥpr-R^c-snb,* justified.'

Bibliography: cf. Davies & Macadam, *Corpus,* no. 100; Daressy, *Recueil,* no. 38; Petrie, *Season,* pl. 22(17); Legrain, *Répertoire,* 112(201); Lefebvre, *Histoire des grands prêtres,* 233; Hayes, *Scepter* II, 129; Mond in *Ann. Serv.* 6 (1905), 65, 95; Porter & Moss, *Top. Bibl.* I^2, 175 ff.

Note: 1. Davies, *The Tombs of Menkheperrasonb etc.* 1, n.2.

76. MENKHEPERRESONB

6 cones, stamps only (UC 37785-8, 37990-1).
Attributed to tomb 79, Sheikh Abd el-Qurna.[1]
Dynasty XVIII, temp. Tuthmosis III - Amenophis II.

5 lines with dividers: . . .[2] overseer of cattle of Amun, hall-keeper of Amun, *k₃*-priest of the good god, scribe of the offering-table of the lord of the Two Lands, *Mn-ḥpr-R^c-snb,* justified with the great god.'

Bibliography: cf. Davies & Macadam, *Corpus,* no. 388; Daressy, *Recueil,* no. 162; Petrie, *Season,* pl. 23(98); Mond in *Ann. Serv.* 6 (1905), 95; Sethe, *Urk.* IV, 1204 f. (b); Helck, *Materialien,* 30, 47, 227; Porter & Moss, *Top. Bibl.* I^2, 156 f.

Notes: 1. Mond seems to have associated the cone with nearby tomb 86. Examples may well have strayed there. 2. The damaged sign shown by Davies is not apparent in the present examples.

77. MENKHEPERRESONB

1 cone, complete, length 24.2 cm. (UC 37855). Ex-Wellcome Collection.
Attributed to tomb 79, Sheikh Abd el-Qurna.[1]
Dynasty XVIII, temp. Tuthmosis III - Amenophis II.

4 lines with dividers: 'King's scribe, overseer of granaries of Upper and Lower Egypt,
Mn-ḫpr-R^c-snb, justified with the great god.'

Bibliography: cf. Davies & Macadam, *Corpus,* no. 493; Daressy, *Recueil,* no. 185; Mond in
Ann. Serv. 6 (1905), 93 ff. (185); *Aeg. Inschr. Berlin* II, 299 (8779-80); Botti, *Antichita
Cortona,* no. 237, tav. a; Hayes, *Scepter* II, 129; Sethe, *Urk.* IV, 1204 f. (a); Helck, *Materialien,*
30; id. *Verwaltung,* 498; Heyler in *Kêmi* 15 (1959), 92; Porter & Moss, *Top. Bibl.* I², 156 f.

Note: 1. See n. 1 of the previous item.

78. MENTUEMHET

1 cone, stamp only (UC 37822).
Attributed to tomb 34, Asasif.[1]
Dynasty XXV, temp. Taharqa and Psammetikhos I.

4 lines with dividers: 'One revered by Osiris, fourth prophet of Amun, *Mntw-m-ḥ3t,*
justified. His wife, whom he loves, king's acquaintance, mistress of the house, *Wḏ3-rn.s,*
justified.'

Bibliography: cf. Davies & Macadam, *Corpus,* no. 418; Daressy, *Recueil,* no. 202; Petrie,
Season, pl. 23(85); Leclant, *Mentouemhat,* 164 f. (type 9); *Aeg. Inschr. Berlin* II, 298
(7643 etc.); Botti, *Antichita Cortona,* no. 243, tav. c, no. 251, tav. d; Porter & Moss,
Top. Bibl. I², 56 ff.

Note: 1. See also the following four items.

79. MENTUEMHET

1 cone, stamp only (UC 37823).
Attributed to tomb 34, Asasif.
Dynasty XXV, temp. Taharqa and Psammetikhos I.

4 lines with dividers: 'One revered by Osiris, fourth prophet of Amun, *Mntw-m-ḥ3t,*
justified. His wife, whom he loves, king's acquaintance, mistress of the house, *Ns-Ḫnsw,*
justified.'

Bibliography: cf. Davies & Macadam, *Corpus,* no. 419; Leclant, *Mentouemhat,* 163 f.
(type 7).

80. MENTUEMHET

1 cone, stamp only, damaged (UC 37853).
Attributed to tomb 34, Asasif.
Dynasty XXV, temp. Taharqa and Psammetikhos I.

4 lines with dividers: 'Fourth prophet of Amun, overseer of Upper Egypt, *Mntw-m-ḥ3t,*
justified. His eldest son of his body, prophet of Amun, king's acquaintance, *Ns-Ptḥ,* son
of the mistress of the house, *Ns-Ḥnsw,* justified.'

Bibliography: cf. Davies & Macadam, *Corpus,* no. 485; Daressy, *Recueil,* no. 174; Petrie,
Season, pl. 23(90); Leclant, *Mentouemhat,* 161 (type 3); *Aeg. Inschr. Berlin* II, 299 (8733-
5); Heyler in *Kêmi* 15 (1959), 92.

81. MENTUEMHET

1 cone, stamp only (UC 37854).
Attributed to tomb 34, Asasif.
Dynasty XXV, temp. Taharqa and Psammetikhos I.

4 lines with dividers: 'Fourth prophet of Amun, mayor of the city, *Mntw-m-ḥ3t,* justified,
son of the prophet of Amun, scribe of the offering-table of the temple of Amun, mayor of
the city, *Ns-Ptḥ,* justified.'

Bibliography: cf. Davies & Macadam, *Corpus,* no. 486; Daressy, *Recueil,* no. 175; Petrie,
Season, pl. 23(91); Leclant, *Mentouemhat,* 162 (type 4).

82. MENTUEMHET

1 cone, stamp only (UC 37977).
Attributed to tomb 34, Asasif.
Dynasty XXV, temp. Taharqa and Psammetikhos I.

3 columns with dividers and 2 kneeling figures beneath solar barque. 'The Osiris, nomarch,
overseer of Upper Egypt, *Mntw-m-ḥ3t,* justified. The Osiris, fourth prophet of Amun,
Mntw-m-ḥ3t, justified.'

Bibliography: cf. Davies & Macadam, *Corpus,* no. 604; Daressy, *Recueil,* no. 260; Leclant,
Mentouemhat, 165 (type 10); *Aeg. Inschr. Berlin* II, 302 (8737).

83. MERUATUM

1 cone, stamp only, damaged (UC 37577).
From West Thebes. Tomb unidentified.
Dynasty XVIII.

4 columns with dividers: 'The Osiris, overseer of horses of the king in Upper and Lower Egypt, *Mrw-'Itm*, justified.'

Bibliography: cf. Davies & Macadam, *Corpus,* no. 97; Daressy, *Recueil,* no. 37; Petrie, *Season,* pl 21 (16); Helck, *Militärführer,* 60; Ranke, *Personennamen* I, 421(19).

84. MERY

11 cones, stamps only (UC 37789-99).
Attributed to tomb 95, Sheikh Abd el-Qurna.[1]
Dynasty XVIII, temp. Amenophis II.

5 lines with dividers: '[Chancellor of][2] the king of Lower Egypt, overseer of prophets of Upper and Lower Egypt, high-priest of Amun, *Mry.* Steward of Amun, overseer of granaries of Amun, *Mry.* Overseer of the treasury, overseer of the gold-houses of Amun, *Mry.* Overseer of cattle of Amun, *Mry.*'

Bibliography: cf. Davies & Macadam, *Corpus,* no. 390; Daressy, *Recueil,* no. 160; Petrie, *Season,* pl. 23(96); Legrain, *Répertoire,* 90(166); Lefebvre, *Histoire des grands prêtres,* 236; Hayes, *Scepter* II, 147; Helck, *Urk.* IV, 1414; id. *Materialien,* 29 f., 33; Porter & Moss, *Top. Bibl.* I[2], 195 ff.

Notes: 1. See also the following item. 2. The sign *sḏȝwty* appears to be missing.

85. MERY

14 cones, stamps only (UC 37802-15).
Attributed to tomb 95, Sheikh Abd el-Qurna.
Dynasty XVIII, temp. Amenophis II.

5 lines with dividers: '[Seal-bearer of][1] the king of Lower Egypt, high-priest of Amun, *Mry.* Overseer of prophets of Upper and Lower Egypt, *Mry.* Overseer of fields of Amun, overseer of granaries of Amun, *Mry.* Possessor of the seal in the palace of the king (life, prosperity, health!), *Mry.* Overseer of cattle of Amun, *Mry.*'

53

Bibliography: cf. Davies & Macadam, *Corpus,* no. 400; Daressy, *Recueil,* no. 161; Petrie, *Season,* pl. 23(97); Legrain, *Répertoire,* 90(166); Lefebvre, *Histoire des grands pretres,* 236; Helck, *Urk.* IV, 1414 f.; id. *Materialien,* 30, 33 f.; Heyler in *Kemi* 15 (1959), 91; Droste von & Schlick-Nolte, *CAA: Rhein-Main* I, 1,109 f.

86. MERY

3 cones, stamps only (UC 37871-3).
From West Thebes. Tomb unidentified.
New Kingdom.

3 lines with dividers: 'One revered by Osiris, scribe of the treasury of Amun, *Mry.*'

Bibliography: cf. Davies & Macadam, *Corpus,* no. 505; Daressy, *Recueil,* no. 239; Petrie, *Season,* pl. 23(76); Northampton etc. *Theban Necropolis,* pl. 24(26); Helck, *Materialien,* 43.

87. MERY

1 cone, stamp only, damaged (UC 37972).
From West Thebes. Tomb unidentified.
New Kingdom.

2 columns, undivided, before kneeling figure: 'Steward of the god's-wife *Mry.*'

Bibliography: cf. Davies & Macadam, *Corpus,* no. 581; Daressy, *Recueil,* no. 134; Helck, *Materialien,* 123.

88. MERYMOSE

16 cones, including 2 complete, max. length 16.4 cm. (UC 37620-33, 37979-80). These include 2 bought in Armant (UC 37632-3)[1] and 2 from the Brunton Collection (UC 37979-80).
Attributed to tomb 383, Qurnet Murai, where many other examples were found.[2]
Dynasty XVIII; the owner was a son of Amenophis III.

3 columns with dividers: 'One revered by Osiris, king's son of Kush, *Mry-ms.*'

Bibliography: cf. Davies & Macadam, *Corpus,* no. 170; Daressy, *Recueil,* no. 113; Petrie, *Season,* pl. 22(29); Legrain, *Répertoire,* 133(233); Mond & Myers, *Temples of Armant,* 101

(P. 1454, 1457); Gauthier, *Livre des rois* II, 337(7); *Aeg. Inschr. Berlin* II, 290 (541 etc.); Botti, *Antichita Cortona,* no. 242, tav. a; Hilton Price, *Catalogue,* 218 (nos. 2030-1); Hayes, *Scepter* II, 276; Droste von & Schlick-Nolte, *CAA: Rhein-Main* I, 1,107 f.; Porter & Moss, *Top. Bibl.* I², 436 f.

Notes: 1. Mond & Myers, loc. cit. 2. Gauthier in *BIFAO* 16 (1919), 167 ff.

89. MERYREMETJEF

1 cone, stamp only, damaged (UC 37560).
Duplicate found in courtyard of unrelated tomb 86, Sheikh Abd el-Qurna.[1] Source unidentified.
Dynasty XVIII.

4 columns with dividers: 'One revered by Osiris, captain of sailors of[2] the high-priest of Amun, *Mry-rmt̠.f.* Mistress of the house, *Mwt.'*

Bibliography: cf. Davies & Macadam, *Corpus,* no. 55; Daressy, *Recueil,* no. 54; Petrie, *Season,* pl. 21(8); Helck, *Materialien,* 52; Schulman, *Military Rank,* 154 (429).

Notes: 1. Mond in *Ann. Serv.* 6 (1905), 95. 2. The genitive *n,* lost in Davies' copy, is preserved in Daressy's and in the present example.

90. MERYREMETJEF

1 cone, stamp only, damaged (UC 37830).
From West Thebes. Tomb unidentified.
New Kingdom.

4 lines with dividers: 'King's butler, page, singer of Amun, *Mry-rmt̠.f.'*

Bibliography: cf. Davies & Macadam, *Corpus,* no. 452; Daressy, *Recueil,* no. 183; Petrie, *Season,* pl. 23(94); Helck, *Materialien,* 50.

91. MIN

1 cone, stamp only, much abraded (UC 37586).
Attributed to tomb 109, Sheikh Abd el-Qurna.[1]
Dynasty XVIII, temp. Tuthmosis III.

4 columns without dividers: 'Mayor of Thinis, overseer of prophets of Onuris, scribe, *Mnw,* justified with the great god.'

Bibliography: cf. Davies & Macadam, *Corpus,* no. 109; Daressy, *Recueil,* no. 74; Petrie, *Season,* pl. 22(50); Hayes, *Scepter* II, 129.

Note: 1. Porter & Moss, *Top. Bibl.* I², 226 f. Other examples found in the courtyard of the neighbouring tomb 23; see Collins L. in *JEA* 62 (1976), 34.

92. MINMONTU

5 cones, stamps only (UC 37666-70).
From West Thebes. Tomb unidentified.
Dynasty XVIII/XIX.

3 columns without dividers: 'Seal-bearer of the king of Lower Egypt, high-priest of Amun, *Mnw-Mntw* called *Sn. i-rs,* justified.'

Bibliography: cf. Davies & Macadam, *Corpus,* no. 245; Daressy, *Recueil,* no. 75; Petrie, *Season,* pl. 22(52); Legrain, *Répertoire,* 7 f.(12); Northampton etc. *Theban Necropolis,* pl. 24(13); Ranke, *Personennamen* I, 152(2).

93. MINMOSE

1 brick, 16.5 x 9.0 x 8.8 cm. with stamp on side and end, much abraded (UC 37978).
From West Thebes. Tomb unidentified.
New Kingdom(?).

A rectangular frame containing seated figures of a man and a woman before an offering-table with 3+ columns of inscription: '... *Mnw-ms* ... eternity ...' In 2 lines on the right: 'Words spoken: revered by you, Osiris. Words spoken: revered by you, Anubis.'

Bibliography: cf. Davies & Macadam, *Corpus,* no. 611; Daressy, *Recueil,* no. 296; Petrie, *Season,* pl. 23(100).

94. MINNAKHT

1 cone, stamp only, damaged (UC 37569).
Attributed to tomb 87, Sheikh Abd el-Qurna.[1]
Dynasty XVIII, temp. Tuthmosis III.

4 columns with dividers: 'Overseer of the throne-room(?)[2], king's scribe, *Mnw-nḫt*, says: I do not utter falsehood, I do no evil.'[3]

Bibliography: cf. Davies & Macadam, *Corpus,* no. 87; Daressy, *Recueil* no. 24; Petrie, *Season,* pl. 22(22); Sethe, *Urk.* IV, 1179 f.(C); Porter & Moss, *Top. Bibl.* I[2], 178 f.

Notes: 1. See also the following item. 2. For the various meanings of *st wrt* see Spencer P. *The Egyptian Temple,* 108 ff. 3. *bw ḏw* confirmed by Daressy and the present example.

95. MINNAKHT

1 cone, complete, length 19.4 cm. (UC 37570).
Attributed to tomb 87, Sheikh Abd el-Qurna.
Dynasty XVIII, temp. Tuthmosis III.

4 columns with dividers: 'Overseer of granaries of Upper and Lower Egypt, *Mnw-nḫt,* says: I am not deaf[1] to the word of truth.'

Bibliography: cf. Davies & Macadam, *Corpus,* no. 89; Daressy, *Recueil,* no. 25; Hayes, *Scepter* II, 128; Sethe, *Urk.* IV, 1179 f.(A).

Note: 1. One might expect the 'ear' determinative in place of the 'walking legs' (correctly copied).

96. NEBENHAU

2 cones, stamps only (UC 37958-9).
Duplicate found at Dra Abu el-Naga.[1] Tomb unidentified.
Dynasty XVIII.

3 lines without dividers: 'King's scribe, *Nb-n-ḥ ꜥ ꜣw* called *'Iꜣ.*'

Bibliography: cf. Davies & Macadam, *Corpus,* no. 550; Daressy, *Recueil,* no. 214; Petrie, *Season,* pl. 22(69); Ranke, *Personennamen* I, 185(11); Heyler in *Kêmi* 15 (1959), 93.

Note: 1. Heyler, ibid 87, n.2 (Strasbourg 382).

97. NEBMEHYT

9 cones, including 3 complete, max. length 21.5 cm. (UC 37862-70).

Duplicate found near unrelated tomb 51, Sheikh Abd el-Qurna.[1] Source unidentified. New Kingdom.

3 lines with dividers: 'One revered by Osiris, scribe, overseer of fields, *Nb-mḥyt*.'

Bibliography: cf. Davies & Macadam, *Corpus,* no. 504; Daressy, *Recueil,* no. 243; Petrie, *Season,* pl. 23(75); Mond & Emery in *Liv. Ann.* 14 (1927), 17, fig. 4; Botti, *Antichita Cortona,* no. 245, tav. b.

Note: Mond in *Ann. Serv.* 6 (1905), 96.

98. NEBNETERU

1 cone, stamp only, broken at top right (UC 37596).
From West Thebes. Tomb unidentified.
New Kingdom.

4 columns with dividers: 'Accountant of cattle of Amun, *Nb-nṯrw*[1], justified with Osiris.'

Bibliography: cf. Davies & Macadam, *Corpus,* no. 127; Daressy, *Recueil,* no. 28; Petrie, *Season,* pl. 22(19); Helck, *Materialien,* 32.

Note: 1. Perhaps the owner of Turin statue no. 3052; see Porter & Moss, *Top. Bibl.* I[2], 794.

99. NEBSENY

1 cone, stamp only (UC 37735).
Attributed to tomb 108, Sheikh Abd el-Qurna.
Dynasty XVIII, temp. Tuthmosis IV(?).

2 columns without dividers in square frame: 'High-priest of Onuris, *Nb-sny*.'

Bibliography: cf. Davies & Macadam, *Corpus,* no. 298; Hayes, *Scepter* II, 154; Helck, *Materialien,* 169; Porter & Moss, *Top. Bibl.* I[2], 225 f.

100. NEDJEM

4 cones, including 1 complete, length 26.0 cm. (UC 37662-5).

Many examples found at Qurnet Murai.[1] The present ones bought at Armant. Tomb unidentified.
Dynasty XVIII.

3 columns with dividers: 'Chief lector-priest of Akheperenre (Tuthmosis II), justified, *Nḏm,* justified.'

Bibliography: cf. Davies & Macadam, *Corpus,* no. 232; Helck, *Materialien,* 90. Mond & Myers, *Temples of Armant,* 101 (P.1447-8, 1450-1), pl. 107.8 (P.1448). See also the following item.

Note: 1. Gauthier in *BIFAO* 16 (1919), 184 f.

101. NEDJEM

3 cones, including 1 complete, length 23.7 cm. (UC 37645-7).
Bought at Armant. From West Thebes. Tomb unidentified.
Dynasty XVIII.

3 columns with dividers: 'Overseer of the storehouse of Akheper(en)re (Tuthmosis II), justified, *Nḏm*[1], justified.'

Bibliography: cf. Davies & Macadam, *Corpus,* no. 193; Helck, *Materialien,* 98. Mond & Myers, *Temples of Armant,* 101 (P.1446, 1449, 1458), pl. 107.9 (P.1449).

Note: 1. Helck, following Davies & Macadam, read the name as ꜥꜣ-bꜣw, but the resemblance to the previous item is so close that they must have belonged to the same man. The fact that both sets of cones were bought at Armant can hardly be a coincidence.

102. NEFERABET

2 cones, stamps only, damaged (UC 37816-7).
From West Thebes. Tomb unidentified.
New Kingdom.

4 lines with dividers: 'One revered by Osiris, overseer of fields of Amun, chief bee-keeper of Amun, wꜥb-priest, *Nfr-ꜥbt,* justified.'

Bibliography: cf. Davies & Macadam, *Corpus,* no. 405; Daressy, *Recueil,* no. 212; Petrie, *Season,* pl. 23(87); Helck, *Materialien,* 34, 41; Haeffner in *Archiv Orientalni* 20 (1952), 610 f., fig. 2.

103. NEFERHEBEF

3 cones, stamps only (UC 37557-9).
From West Thebes. Tomb unidentified.
Dynasty XVIII.

4 columns with dividers: 'One revered by Osiris, prophet of Akheperure (Amenophis II),
given life, *Nfr-ḥb.f*[1], justified. His sister, mistress of the house, *T3-w3y.*'

Bibliography: cf. Davies & Macadam, *Corpus,* no. 54; Daressy, *Recueil,* no. 55; Petrie,
Season, pl. 21(6); Helck, *Materialien,* 98; Hayes, *Scepter* II, 142.

Note: 1. For a second prophet of Amenophis II with the same name see Porter & Moss,
Top. Bibl. I², 789.

104. NEFERHEBEF

2 cones, stamps only (UC 37654-5).
From West Thebes. Tomb unidentified.
New Kingdom.

3 columns with dividers: 'The Osiris, scribe of the high-priest of Amun, *Nfr-ḥb.f,*
justified.'

Bibliography: cf. Davies & Macadam, *Corpus,* no. 216; Helck, *Materialien,* 52.

105. NEFERHOTEP

1 cone, stamp only (UC 37736).
Duplicate found in courtyard of tomb 50[1], and another in pit of unrelated tomb 21[2], both
at Sheikh Abd el-Qurna.
Dynasty XVIII.

2 columns without dividers: 'Fourth prophet of Amun, *Nfr-ḥtp,* justified.'

Bibliography: cf. Davies & Macadam, *Corpus,* no. 301; Daressy, *Recueil,* no. 136; *Aeg.
Inschr. Berlin* II, 297 (7252 etc.); James, *Corpus Brooklyn,* no. 200; Kees, *Priestertum,*
76, n.3.

Notes: 1. Collins L. in *JEA* 62 (1976), 32. It is doubtful if the owner of tomb 50, also
a Neferhotep, was the same man. 2. Mond in *Ann. Serv.* 6 (1905), 95.

106. NEFERIOH

1 cone, stamp only (UC 37585).
From West Thebes. Tomb unidentified.
New Kingdom.

4 columns with dividers: 'For the *ka* of the high-priest of Ioh, *Nfr-'T͗h*, justified, revered, (in) peace. Mistress of the house, musician of Amun, singer of Mut, *Hmt-ntr*, justified, in peace.'

Bibliography: cf. Davies & Macadam, *Corpus,* no. 107; Daressy, *Recueil,* no. 32; Petrie, *Season,* pl. 22(24); Helck, *Materialien,* 62.

107. NEFERMIN

1 cone, stamp only (UC 37874).
From West Thebes. Tomb unidentified.
New Kingdom.

3 lines with dividers: 'One revered by Osiris, scribe of the temple of Seth, *Nfr-Mnw*, justified.'

Bibliogrpahy: cf. Davies & Macadam, *Corpus,* no. 506; Daressy, *Recueil,* no. 244; Petrie, *Season* pl. 23(73); Helck, *Materialien,* 162.

108. NEFERRONPET

6 cones, stamps only, and 1 brick, wedge-shaped, 14.0 x 13.2 x 5.7 cm., with 2 stamps on one face and 1 stamp on end (UC 37605-11).
Attributed to tomb 249, Sheikh Abd el-Qurna.
Dynasty XVIII, temp. Tuthmosis IV(?).

3 columns with dividers: 'One revered by Osiris, purveyor of date-wine, *Nfr-rnpt.*'

Bibliography: cf. Davies & Macadam, *Corpus,* no. 153; Daressy, *Recueil,* no. 115; Petrie, *Season,* pl. 22(36); Northampton etc. *Theban Necropolis,* pl. 25(44); Hayes, *Scepter* II, 276; Porter & Moss, *Top. Bibl.* I², 335.

109. NENTAWAREF

1 cone, stamp only (UC 37521).
Attributed to tomb 398, Sheikh Abd el-Qurna.
Dynasty XVIII(?).

5 columns with dividers: 'One revered by Osiris, page, overseer of $w^c b$-priests of Amun, *Nn-t3-w3-r.f,* justified.'

Bibliography: cf. Davies & Macadam, *Corpus,* no. 13; Daressy, *Recueil,* no. 116; Petrie, *Season,* pl. 22(30); Hayes, *Scepter* II, 325; Porter & Moss, *Top. Bibl.* I², 443.

110. NERAU

1 cone, complete, length 34.5 cm. (UC 37731).
From West Thebes. Tomb unidentified.
Dynasty XVIII.

2 columns with dividers: 'King's butler, *Nr3w.*'

Bibliography: cf. Davies & Macadam, *Corpus,* no. 277; Ranke, *Personennamen* I, 424 (16).

111. NETERMOSE

3 cones, stamps only (UC 37561-3).
From West Thebes. Tomb unidentified.
New Kingdom.

4 columns with dividers: 'One revered by Osiris, scribe of the offering-table of the lord of the Two Lands, *Ntr-ms.*'

Bibliography: cf. Davies & Macadam, *Corpus,* no. 62; Daressy, *Recueil,* no. 41; Petrie, *Season,* pl. 21(11).

112. PABASA

1 cone, stamp only (UC 37840).
Attributed to tomb 279, Asasif (see also the following item).
Dynasty XXVI, temp. Psammetikhos I.

4 lines with dividers: 'The Osiris, prophet of Amen-Re, king of the gods, overseer of prophets of the gods of Upper Egypt, overseer of all Upper Egypt, chief steward of the divine votaress, *P3-b3-s3*, son of the beloved of the god, *P3-di-B3stt*, his mother being *T3-snt-Hr.*'

Bibliography: cf. Davies & Macadam, *Corpus*, no. 468; Daressy, *Recueil*, no. 191; Brunner-Traut & Brunner, *Ägyptische Sammlung Tübingen*, 32(1698), Taf. 124, lower right; Porter & Moss, *Top. Bibl.* I², 357 ff.

113. PABASA

2 cones, stamps only (UC 37841-2).
Attributed to tomb 279, Asasif.
Dynasty XXVI, temp. Psammetikhos I.

4 lines with dividers: 'The Osiris, prophet of Amen-Re, king of the gods, overseer of prophets of the gods of Upper Egypt, overseer of all Upper Egypt, chief steward of the divine votaress, *P3-b3-s3*, justified, son of the beloved of the god, *P3-di-B3stt*, his mother being the mistress of the house, *T3-snt-Hr*, justified.'

Bibliography: cf. Davies & Macadam, *Corpus*, no. 469; Daressy, *Recueil*, no. 181.

114. PAHEKAMEN

1 cone, stamp only (UC 37829).
Attributed to tomb 343 Sheikh Abd el-Qurna.
Early Dynasty XVIII.

4 lines with dividers: 'Overseer of works, page, *P3-hk3-mn* called *Bni3*, justified with Osiris.'

Bibliography: cf. Davies & Macadam, *Corpus*, no. 441; Porter & Moss, *Top. Bibl.* I², 410 ff.

115. PASER

2 cones, stamps only, damaged (UC 37592-3).
From West Thebes. Tomb unidentified.
New Kingdom.

4 columns with dividers: 'King's scribe, steward of Amun in the granary of the divine offerings, *P3-sr.*'

Bibliography: cf. Davies & Macadam, *Corpus,* no 125; Daressy, *Recueil,* no. 23; Petrie, *Season,* pl. 22(18); Helck, *Materialien,* 30, 55; id. in *OLZ* 1959, 371.

116. PASER

2 cones, stamps only, damaged (UC 37594-5).
From West Thebes, possibly from the same tomb as the previous item.
New Kingdom.

4 columns with dividers: 'Overseer of granaries of Upper and Lower Egypt, king's scribe . . .[1] *P3-sr,* justified.'

Bibliography: cf. Davies & Macadam, *Corpus,* no. 126; Daressy, *Recueil,* no. 29; Petrie, *Season,* pl. 22(28).

Note: 1. Signs lost in all available examples.

117. PASER

2 cones, stamps only (UC 37660-1).
Attributed to tomb 367, Sheikh Abd el-Qurna.
Dynasty XVIII, temp. Amenophis II.

3 columns with dividers: 'Chief retainer, chief bowman, page, *P3-sr*[1], justified.'

Bibliography: cf. Davies & Macadam, *Corpus,* no. 230; Daressy, *Recueil,* no. 85; Petrie, *Season,* pl. 22(41); Helck, *Urk.* IV, 1457; Porter & Moss, *Top. Bibl.* I[2], 430 f.

Note: 1. Misread as *P3-wr* in Davies & Macadam.

118. PASINESU

1 cone, stamp only (UC 37754).
From West Thebes. Tomb unidentified.
New Kingdom.

2 columns without dividers in oval frame: 'Chief deputy (?) of the palace of his Majesty, *P3-s3-nsw.'*

Bibliography: cf. Davies & Macadam, *Corpus,* no. 309; Daressy, *Recueil,* no. 280.

119. PAWERIT

1 cone, stamp only (UC 37658).
From West Thebes. Tomb unidentified.
New Kingdom.

3 columns without dividers: 'Nomarch, scribe of the offering-table of the lord of the Two Lands, *P3-wr-ỉt.* (Dedicated) by his son, scribe, *Mry.*'

Bibliography: cf. Davies & Macadam, *Corpus,* no. 221; Daressy, *Recueil,* no. 71; Petrie, *Season,* pl. 22(51).

120. PEDIHORRESNET

1 cone, stamp only, much abraded (UC 37944).
Attributed to tomb 196, Asasif, where many examples found.[1]
Dynasty XXVI, temp. Necho II.

3 lines with dividers: 'Hereditary noble, nomarch, chief steward of the divine votaress, *P3-dỉ-Ḥr-rsnt,* son of the overseer of chamberlains of the divine votaress, *3ḫt-'Imn-ỉrw.*'

Bibliography: cf. Davies & Macadam, *Corpus,* no. 515; Daressy, *Recueil,* no. 218; Porter & Moss, *Top. Bibl.* I², 302; pt. 2, xxii (Addenda).

Note: 1. 'Fouilles de l'Assassif 1970-75' in *Chron. d'Égypte* 50 (1975), 23 ff., particularly 33.

121. PENAMUN

1 brick, 5.9 x 3.8 x 3.7 cm. with single stamp (UC 37768).
Duplicate found in courtyard of unrelated tomb 81, Sheikh Abd el-Qurna.[1] Source unidentified.
New Kingdom.

1 column in rectangular frame: 'Page, *P3-n-'Imn.*'

Bibliography: cf. Davies & Macadam, *Corpus,* no. 341; Daressy, *Recueil,* no. 292; Petrie, *Season,* pl. 22(61).

Note: 1. Mond in *Ann. Serv.* 6 (1905), 96.

122. PENRE

1 cone, stamp only, damaged (UC 37828).
Other examples from Sheikh Abd el-Qurna.[1] Tomb unidentified.
Early Dynasty XVIII.

4 lines with dividers: 'Steward, overseer of cattle of Akheperkare (Tuthmosis I), scribe, *P3-n-R^c*, justified with the great god, lord of the necropolis.'

Bibliography: cf. Davies & Macadam, *Corpus,* no. 438; Daressy, *Recueil,* no. 171 (without dividers and differing in some details); Sethe, *Urk.* IV, 129; Hayes, *Scepter* II, 77 f.

Note: 1. Legrain, *Répertoire,* 46 f.(74); Mond in *Ann. Serv.* 6 (1905), 95 (the latter example from the courtyard of tomb 81).

123. PENRE

7 cones, points missing (UC 37947-53).
Other examples found on sites of tomb 346[1] (probably usurped from Penre) and unrelated tomb 124[2], both at Sheikh Abd el-Qurna.
Dynasty XIX, temp. Ramesses II(?).

3 lines with dividers: 'Chief of the Medjay, overseer of the lands of Syria, charioteer of his Majesty, *P(3)-n-R^c*, justified.'

Bibliography: cf. Davies & Macadam, *Corpus,* no. 524; Daressy, *Recueil,* no. 228; Mond & Emery in *Liv. Ann.* 14 (1927), 24, fig. 18; Hayes, *Scepter* II, 325; Helck, *Materialien,* 103; Kees, *Priestertum,* 147, n.4.

Notes: 1. Porter & Moss, *Top. Bibl.* I^2, 414. 2. Mond in *Ann. Serv.* 6 (1905), 96.

124. PENTJEBU

1 cone, stamp only (UC 37943).
Duplicate found at Dra Abu el-Naga.[1] Tomb unidentified.
Dynasty XVIII.

3 lines without dividers: 'Steward, *P3-n-ṯbw,* justified.'

Bibliography: cf. Davies & Macadam, *Corpus,* no. 509; Daressy, *Recueil,* no. 227 (with dividers and differing in detail); Northampton etc. *Theban Necropolis,* pl. 25(38); Heyler in *Kêmi* 15 (1959), 92.

Note: 1. Heyler, ibid. 87, n.2 (Strasbourg 406).

125. PIA

2 cones, stamps only (UC 37514-5).
Attributed to tomb 344, Dra Abu el-Naga.
Other examples found in courtyard of tomb 23, Sheikh Abd el-Qurna.[1]
Ramesside.

5 columns with dividers: 'One revered by Osiris, overseer of horses, overseer of cattle
of Amun, *Pἰꜣ*, justified. (Dedicated) by his son, overseer of cattle of Amun, *S(-n)-wꜣst*,
justified.'

Bibliography: cf. Davies & Macadam, *Corpus,* no. 6; Daressy, *Recueil,* no. 7; Petrie,
Season, pl. 21(15); Hayes, *Scepter* II, 429; Helck, *Materialien,* 31; Porter & Moss, *Top. Bibl.*
I², 412 f.

Note: 1. Collins L. in *JEA* 62 (1976), 34 f.

126. PIA

2 cones, stamps only (UC 37965-6).
Other examples found in courtyard of unrelated tomb 23, Sheikh Abd el-Qurna.[1] Source
unidentified.
New Kingdom.

3 lines with dividers: 'Scribe of offerings of the king, *Pἰꜣ.* His wife, mistress of the house,
Nḏmt.'

Bibliography: cf. Davies & Macadam, *Corpus,* no. 562; Daressy, *Recueil,* no. 226; Petrie,
Season, pl. 23(79).

Note: 1. Collins, loc. cit.

127. RAMOSE

2 cones, complete, lengths 8.9 and 15.0 cm. (UC 37510-1).
Attributed to tomb 132, Sheikh Abd el-Qurna.
Dynasty XXV, temp. Taharqa.

6 columns with dividers: 'King's scribe, seal-bearer of the king of Lower Egypt, beloved sole companion, eyes of the king of Upper Egypt, ears of the king of Lower Egypt, overseer of the treasury of the lord of the Two Lands, Taharqa, justified, R^c-*ms,* justified, born of the mistress of the house, *Ṯs-mḥyt-prt,* justified.'

Bibliography: cf. Davies & Macadam, *Corpus,* no. 3; Daressy, *Recueil,* no. 2; *Aeg. Inschr. Berlin* II, 297 (540 etc.); Porter & Moss, *Top. Bibl* I², 247.

128. RAMOSE

1 cone, stamp only (UC 37597).
Attributed to tomb 55, Sheikh Abd el-Qurna.[1]
Dynasty XVIII, temp. Amenophis IV.

4 columns with dividers: 'Thou adorest Re at dawn, hereditary noble, sole companion, foremost of the great ones, overseer of the city, vizier, R^c-*ms,* justified.'

Bibliography: cf. Davies & Macadam, *Corpus,* no. 133; Daressy, *Recueil,* no. 31; Hayes, *Scepter* II, 276; Helck, *Urk.* IV, 1791; id. *Verwaltung,* 443; Porter & Moss, *Top. Bibl* I², 105 ff.

Note: 1. See also Davies & Macadam no. 132.

129. RE

1 brick, wedge-shaped, fragment only, length 18.5 cm. with 2 stamps on one side and another on end (UC 37839).
Attributed to tomb 201, Khokha.
Dynasty XVIII, temp. Tuthmosis IV - Amenophis III.

4 lines with dividers: 'The Osiris, chief king's herald of the lord of the Two Lands, one praised by the good god, trusty confidant, R^c.

Bibliography: cf. Davies & Macadam, *Corpus,* no. 466; Daressy, *Recueil,* no. 198; Petrie, *Season,* pl. 23(88); Hayes, *Scepter* II, 129; Helck, *Urk.* IV, 1640; Porter & Moss, *Top.Bibl.* I², 304 f.

130. RENWY

2 cones, stamps only (UC 37672-3).
From West Thebes. Tomb unidentified.
New Kingdom.

3 columns without dividers: 'Chantress[1] of Amun, *Rnwy, W*^{r}*b*-priest, *'Imn-ḥtp.'*

Bibliography: cf. Davies & Macadam, *Corpus,* no. 247; Helck in *OLZ* 1959, 371.

Note: 1. Helck amends *ḥrwfyt*(?) in Davies & Macadam to *šm*^{r}*yt.*

131. RURU

4 cones, stamps only (UC 37612-5).
Attributed to tomb A.3, Dra Abu el-Naga. Many examples found in that area.[1]
New Kingdom.

3 columns without dividers: 'One revered by Osiris, chief of the Medjay, *Rr,* justified.'

Bibliography: cf. Davies & Macadam, *Corpus,* no. 158; Daressy, *Recueil,* no. 106; Petrie, *Season,* pl. 22(48); Porter & Moss, *Top. Bibl.* I², 447.

Note: 1. Gauthier in *BIFAO* 6 (1908), 128 f.

132. SEBEKMOSE

2 cones, points missing (UC 37858-9).
Bought at Armant. From West Thebes. Tomb unidentified.
Dynasty XVIII.

3 lines with dividers: 'One revered by Osiris, chief *w*^{r}*b*-priest, *Sbk-ms,* justified.'

Bibliography: cf. Davies & Macadam, *Corpus,* no. 501; Hayes, *Scepter* II, 276. Mond & Myers, *Temples of Armant,* 101 (P.1453, 1455).

133. SEBEKNAKHT

1 cone, stamp only (UC 37603).
Other examples found at Qurnet Murai.[1] Tomb unidentified.
Dynasty XVIII.

3 columns with dividers: 'One revered by Osiris, steward of Amun, *Sbk-nḫt.'*

Bibliography: cf. Davies & Macadam, *Corpus,* no. 144; Daressy, *Recueil,* no. 117; Hayes, *Scepter* II, 276; Helck, *Urk.* IV, 1889; id. *Militärführer,* 32.

Note: 1. Gauthier in *BIFAO* 16 (1919), 169 ff.

134. SENEMIOH

1 brick, 29.3 x 13.0 x 8.8 cm. with 1 stamp on face and 1 on each end (UC 37856).
Attributed to tomb 127, Sheikh Abd el-Qurna.
Dynasty XVIII, temp. Tuthmosis III(?).

4 lines without dividers: 'Accountant of grain of Upper and Lower Egypt, *Sn-m-iᶜḫ,* justified with the great god.'

Bibliography: cf. Davies & Macadam, *Corpus,* no. 494; Helck, *Verwaltung,* 509; Porter & Moss, *Top. Bibl.* I², 241 ff.

135. SENHOTEP

2 cones, stamps only (UC 37762-3).
From West Thebes. Tomb unidentified.
New Kingdom.

2 columns without dividers: 'Scribe of the cadaster, *Sn-ḥtp.'*

Bibliography: cf. Davies & Macadam, *Corpus,* no. 320.

136. SENISONB

2 cones, stamps only (UC 37758-9). Sides of cone slightly flattened.
From West Thebes. Tomb unidentified.
New Kingdom.

2 columns without dividers in square frame: 'His sister, whom he loves, mistress of the house, *Sn. i-snb.'*[1]

Bibliography: cf. Davies & Macadam, *Corpus,* no. 312.

Note: 1. This cone was obviously intended to accompany another with the tomb-owner's name.

137. SENNETER

2 cones, stamps only (UC 37638-9).
Duplicate found in courtyard of unrelated tomb 23, Sheikh Abd el-Qurna.[1] Source unidentified.
Dynasty XVIII.

3 columns without dividers: 'One revered by Osiris, scribe, *Sn-nṯr*, justified.'

Bibliography: cf. Davies & Macadam, *Corpus*, no. 173; Daressy, *Recueil*, no. 105; Petrie, *Season*, pl. 22(49).

Note: 1. Collins L. in *JEA* 62 (1976), 34.

138. SESHI

3 cones, points missing, interiors hollow (UC 37598-37600).
Other examples found at Dra Abu el-Naga.[1] Tomb unidentified.
New Kingdom.

3 columns without dividers: 'One revered by Anubis, who is upon his mountain, overseer of ships of Amun, *Sši*, justified.'

Bibliography: cf. Davies & Macadam, *Corpus*, no. 138; Helck, *Materialien*, 48.

Note: 1. Gauthier in *BIFAO* 6 (1908), 133 f.

139. SETEKH

1 cone, stamp only, much abraded (UC 37846).
From West Thebes. Tomb unidentified.
New Kingdom.

4 lines with dividers: 'The Osiris, / standard(?) / -bearer . . . *Stḫ* . . .'

Bibliography: cf. Davies & Macadam, *Corpus*, no. 479; Helck in *OLZ* 1959, 373.

140. SIDJEHUTY

3 cones, stamps only, with inscriptions unusually in sunk relief (UC 37968-70).
Duplicate found at Dra Abu el-Naga.[1] Tomb unidentified.
New Kingdom.

2 lines without dividers: 'Fourth prophet of Amun, *S3-Dhwty*, justified.'

Bibliography: cf. Davies & Macadam, *Corpus*, no. 571; Daressy, *Recueil*, no. 254; Petrie, *Season*, pl. 22(66); Northampton etc. *Theban Necropolis*, pl. 24(14); Heyler in *Kêmi* 15 (1959), 93; Kees, *Priestertum*, Nachträge, 27 (S.320).

Note: 1. Heyler, ibid. 87, n.2 (Strasbourg 398).

141. SIESI

1 cone, stamp only, damaged (UC 37674).
From West Thebes. Tomb unidentified.
Dynasty XVIII.

3 columns with dividers: 'Standard-bearer of the king's ship 'Appearing-in-truth', *S3-3st*, justified.'

Bibliography: cf. Davies & Macadam, *Corpus*, no. 249; Daressy, *Recueil*, no. 87; Petrie, *Season*, pl. 22(40); Hayes, *Scepter* II, 276; Schulman, *Military Rank*, 164 (494h).

142. SIMUT

1 cone, stamp only, much abraded (UC 37857).
From West Thebes. Tomb unidentified.
Ramesside.

3 lines with dividers: 'One revered by Osiris, lieutenant-commander of the Medjay, *S3-mwt*.

Bibliography: cf. Davies & Macadam, *Corpus*, 500; Daressy, *Recueil*, no. 245; Petrie, *Season*, pl. 23(77); Hayes, *Scepter* II, 429.

143. SINEH

1 cone, stamp only, damaged, interior hollow (UC 37653).
From West Thebes. Tomb unidentified.
New Kingdom.

3 columns with dividers: 'The Osiris, scribe of the treasury of the lord of the Two Lands, *S3-Nḥ*(?)[1], son of the dignitary[2], *P3-b3k*, born of the mistress of the house, *T3-nfr(t)*, justified.'

Bibliography: cf. Davies & Macadam, *Corpus,* no. 215; Daressy, *Recueil,* no. 99; Petrie, *Season,* pl. 22(38); Fabretti etc. *Regie Museo di Turino* I, 457 (3413-5), tav. 3 (311).

Notes: 1. Not listed in Ranke, *Personennamen,* and queried by Davies & Macadam. Daressy rendered the name as *S3-Mwt,* omitting the breast-tuft on the bird, although the tuft is clearly visible in the present example; the possibility remains that it may have been a flaw in the matrix. 2. For the formula *s3 s3b* see *Wb.* III, 422.

144. SIRE

1 cone, stamp only (UC 37967).
From West Thebes. Tomb unidentified.
New Kingdom.

2 lines without dividers: 'King's butler, *S3-Rꜥ.*'

Bibliography: cf. Davies & Macadam, *Corpus,* no. 567.

145. SIRE

1 cone, stamp only, damaged (UC 37971).[1]
From West Thebes. Tomb unidentified.
New Kingdom.

2 lines without dividers: 'Page, *S3-Rꜥ.*'

Bibliography: cf. Davies & Macadam, *Corpus,* no. 573.

Note: 1. Possibly from the same tomb as the previous item.

146. SUEMNUT

1 cone, stamp only (UC 37641).
Attributed to tomb 92, Sheikh Abd el-Qurna.
Dynasty XVIII, temp. Amenophis II.

3 columns with dividers: 'One revered by Osiris, fan-bearer, *Sw-m-nĭwt*, justified.'

Bibliography: cf. Davies & Macadam, *Corpus,* no. 181; Daressy, *Recueil,* no. 124; Helck, *Urk.* IV, 1452; id. *Militärführer,* 42; Porter & Moss, *Top. Bibl.* I², 187 ff.

147. SURER

3 cones, points missing (UC 37843-5).
Attributed to tomb 48, Khokha.[1] Other examples found at Qurnet Murai.[2] The present three bought at Armant.
Dynasty XVIII, temp. Amenophis III.

4 lines with dividers: 'The Osiris, king's scribe, fan-bearer on the right side of the king, *Swrr*, justified.'

Bibliography: cf. Davies & Macadam, *Corpus,* no. 477; Daressy, *Recueil,* no. 199; Petrie, *Season,* pl. 23(78); Mond & Myers, *Temples of Armant,* 101 (P.1452, 1456, 1459); Säve-Söderbergh, *Four Eighteenth Dynasty Tombs,* 35, pl. 70(c); Hayes, *Scepter* II, 276; Helck, *Urk.* IV, 1907; id. *Militärführer,* 46; id. *Verwaltung,* 482; Porter & Moss, *Top. Bibl.* I², 87 ff.

Notes: 1. The identification has been widely accepted, although Gauthier thought the evidence insufficient; see *BIFAO* 16 (1919), 173 f. 2. Gauthier, ibid.

148. TAHIRSETJANEF

4 cones, stamps only (UC 37517-20).
Other examples found at Dra Abu el-Naga.[1] Tomb unidentified.
Dynasty XVIII.

5 columns with dividers: 'One revered by Osiris, purveyor of date-wine of Amun, *T3-ḥr-stȝ-n.f.* (Dedicated) by his son to perpetuate his name, purveyor of date-wine of Amun, *Ḥry-ĭry*, justified.'

Bibliography: cf. Davies & Macadam, *Corpus,* no. 9; Daressy, *Recueil,* no. 11; Petrie, *Season,* pl. 21(3); Helck, *Materialien,* 41; Heyler in *Kêmi* 15 (1959), 88.

Notes: 1. Heyler, ibid. 87, n.2 (Strasbourg 383). See also the following item. 2. Cf. Ranke, *Personennamen* I, 376(26 var.).

149. TAHIRSETJANEF

3 cones, stamps only (UC 37547-9).
From West Thebes. Tomb unidentified.
Dynasty XVIII.

4 columns with dividers: 'One revered by Osiris, purveyor of date-wine of Amun, *T3-ḥr-st3-n.f*[1], justified.'

Bibliography: cf. Davies & Macadam, *Corpus,* no. 39; Daressy, *Recueil,* no. 58; Petrie, *Season,* pl. 21(4); Northampton etc. *Theban Necropolis,* pl. 25(49); Helck, *Materialien,* 41.

Note: 1. Despite the difference in writing, this is almost certainly the same person as in the previous item.

150. TEPAATEN

2 cones, stamps only (UC 37963-4).
From West Thebes. Tomb unidentified.
Late Dynasty XVIII(?).

3 lines with dividers: 'Scribe of the granary, *T-p3-itn.*'

Bibliography: cf. Davies & Macadam, *Corpus,* no. 561; Daressy, *Recueil,* no. 225; Petrie, *Season,* pl. 23(80); Hayes, *Scepter* II, 325.

151. TER

2 cones, stamps only (UC 37760-1).
From West Thebes. Tomb unidentified.
New Kingdom.

2 columns without dividers: 'Scribe, overseer of fields of the king's wife, *Tr,* justified.'

Bibliography: cf. Davies & Macadam, *Corpus*, no. 313; Daressy, *Recueil*, no. 139; Petrie, *Season*, pl. 22(57); Helck, *Materialien*, 213.

152. TETIEMRE

1 cone, stamp only, right side damaged (UC 37767).
From West Thebes. Tomb unidentified.
Early Dynasty XVIII.

1 column in oval frame: 'Mayor of the city, *Tti-m-R*ᶜ.'

Bibliography: cf. Davies & Macadam, *Corpus*, no. 339; Daressy, *Recueil*, no. 276; Petrie, *Season*, pl. 23(105); Helck, *Verwaltung*, 523.

153. TJAY

1 cone, stamp only, double-stamped (UC 37755).
2 bricks: (a) 11.5 x 6.3 x 5.0 cm. with 2 stamps on one face (UC 37756); (b) 10.4 x 6.6.x 4.5 cm. with 2 stamps on each of 3 faces (UC 37757).
Other examples of cones found at Sheikh Abd el-Qurna.[1] Tomb unidentified.
Ramesside.

2 columns with dividers in oval frame: 'A gift which the king gives to Osiris, lord of eternity, ruler of infinity, who made heaven. Chief merchant (?), *Tȝy*, justified.'

Bibliography: cf. Davies & Macadam, *Corpus*, no. 311; Daressy, *Recueil*, no. 272; Petrie, *Season*, pl. 23(103); Hayes, *Scepter* II, 429.

Note: 1. Collins L. in *JEA* 62 (1976), 35.

154. TY

1 cone, stamp only (UC 37546).
From West Thebes. Tomb unidentified.
New Kingdom.

4 columns with dividers: 'One revered by Osiris, store-keeper of Amun, *Ty*, justified. His sister, whom he loves, mistress of the house, *Mry(t)*, justified, lady of reverence.'

Bibliography: cf. Davies & Macadam, *Corpus*, no. 37; Daressy, *Recueil*, no. 61; Northampton etc. *Theban Necropolis*, pl. 25(33); Helck, *Materialien*, 47.

155. USERHET

1 cone, stamp only (UC 37675).
Attributed to tomb 150, Dra Abu el-Naga, where many other examples found [1], or perhaps to tomb 56, Sheikh Abd el-Qurna[2].
Dynasty.XVIII.

2 columns without dividers: 'Overseer of cattle of Amun, Wsr-ḥ3t.'[3]

Bibliography: cf. Davies & Macadam, *Corpus*, no. 255; Helck, *Materialien*, 30.

Notes: 1. Gauthier in *BIFAO* 6 (1908), 131 f.; Porter & Moss, *Top. Bibl.* I², 261. 2. Helck, loc. cit. 3. See also Davies & Macadam no. 256.

156. USERHET

1 cone, stamp only, damaged (UC 37818).
Attributed to tomb 47, Khokha, where an example found.[1]
Others from courtyard of unrelated tomb 23, Sheikh Abd el-Qurna.[2]
Dynasty XVIII, temp. Amenophis III.

4 lines with dividers: 'One revered by Osiris, overseer of the king's harem, Wsr-ḥ3t, justified, son of the dignitary Nḥ, justified, and of Snnw. (His wife), mistress of the house, whom he loves, Mἰy, justified.'

Bibliography: cf. Davies & Macadam, *Corpus*, no. 406; Daressy, *Recueil*, no. 207; Petrie, *Season*, pl 23(83); Hayes, *Scepter* II, 276; Helck, *Urk.* IV, 1880; Reiser, *Kgl. Harim* . 28, 73; Porter & Moss, *Top. Bibl.* I², 87.

Notes: 1. Carter in *Ann. Serv.* 4 (1903), 177 f., fig. A. 2. Collins in *JEA* 62 (1976), 34.

157. USERHET

2 cones, including 1 complete, length 23.0 cm. (UC 37820-1).
The latter formerly in the Wellcome Collection.
Other examples found at Qurnet Murai.[1] Tomb unidentified.
Dynasty XVIII.

4 lines with dividers: 'One revered by Osiris, wʿb-priest, scribe of the treasury of Amun, Wsr-ḥ3t[2], son of the scribe of the treasury, Nb-wʿw.'[3]

Bibliography: cf. Davies & Macadam, *Corpus,* no. 415; Daressy, *Recueil,* no. 211; Petrie, *Season,* pl. 23(86); Helck, *Materialien,* 43.

Notes: 1. Gauthier in *BIFAO* 16 (1919), 166 f. 2. See also Davies & Macadam no. 63. 3. For a pair-statue of Nebwaw and his wife, dedicated by Userhet, see Hayes, *Scepter* II, 158, fig. 87; Porter & Moss, *Top. Bibl.* I², 792; cf. Gauthier, ibid. (The Hartwell statue group mentioned by Gauthier is the same one). For further bibliography see Helck, loc. cit.

158. USERHET

1 cone, stamp only (UC 37945).
From West Thebes. Tomb unidentified.
New Kingdom.

3 lines without dividers: '*Wᶜb*-priest of Amun, *Wsr-ḥ3t,* son of the nomarch, *'Idḥ-ms.* '¹

Bibliography: cf. Davies & Macadam, *Corpus,* no. 520; Daressy, *Recueil,* no. 217; Petrie, *Season,* pl. 22(68).

Note: 1. Indexed by Macadam as *Tᶜḥ-ms.* The sign *d* is, however, quite clear on the cone.

159. WERSHU

4 cones, points missing (UC 37750-3).
Other examples found at Dra Abu el-Naga.¹ Tomb unidentified.
New Kingdom.

2 stamps in separate oval frames on each cone: (a) 'Chief servant of Amun, *Wršw,* repeating life'; (b) 'His beloved wife, *Ḥnwt,* justified, lady of reverence.'

Bibliography: cf. Davies & Macadam, *Corpus,* nos. 308, 340; Daressy, *Recueil,* nos. 273-4; Helck, *Materialien,* 40; Heyler in *Kêmi* 15 (1959), 89, pi. 13, fig. 2 (left).

Note: 1. Heyler, ibid. 87, n.2 (Strasbourg 377, 389, 395).

160. WESY

64 cones (UC 37875-37938), including 3 complete, max. length 26.4 cm.; 4 wedge-shaped bricks (UC 37939-42), max. 21.0 x 18.5 x 8.2 cm. with 2 stamps on one side and 1 stamp on end.¹

Other examples found at Dra Abu el-Naga.[2] Tomb unidentified.
Dynasty XVIII.

3 lines with dividers: 'One revered by Osiris, accountant of grain of the lord of the Two
Lands, *Wsy*[3], justified.'

Bibliography: cf. Davies & Macadam, *Corpus*, no. 508; Daressy, *Recueil*, no. 240; Petrie,
Season, pl. 23(74).

Notes: 1. Such a large concentration must surely have indicated the position of the tomb.
It is unfortunate that there is no record of the find-spot. 2. Gauthier in *BIFAO* 6 (1908),
129. 3. For a statue of an accountant of grain called *Wsy,* also from Dra Abu el-Naga, see
Porter & Moss, *Top. Bibl.* I[2], 606. Excavated by Petrie (*Qurneh,* 12*[25]*, 17*[39]*, pl. 32)
and now in Boston Museum, it was discovered in the vicinity of tombs 19 and 344, both of
later date.

161. READING AND AUTHENTICITY DOUBTFUL
Plate 25

1 cone, stamp only (UC 37987).
From West Thebes.
New Kingdom.

4 columns with dividers: ' . . . of the king, foremost of this[1] his land, king's eldest son[2],
overseer of granaries of Upper / and Lower / Egypt (?) . . .[3] *Ḳn-Rˁ* (?), son of the
dignitary *Sḥrw* . . . '

Comment: Apart from a few minor differences in copying, this is clearly the same stamp
as Davies & Macadam, *Corpus*, no. 134, which the traces fit. A duplicate cone in the
Ashmolean Museum, Oxford (no. 1972.352), probably the original of Davies' drawing,
serves to allay some initial doubts about the authenticity of the U.C. stamp, which is
unusually regular with suggestions of rilling on the sides. This does not occur in the
Ashmolean example.

Notes: 1. Although the penultimate sign has sloping sides, it is difficult to see what
other interpretation might be placed on this group. 2. *Sꜣ-nsw tpy.* 3. The signs at the
top of the column in Davies' copy (confirmed by the Ashmolean example) suggest the
restoration *sḫm* (or *ˁḥˁ* ?) *tpy m ḥms,* although such an epithet would be very odd. The
squatting figure is clear on the present stamp, and does not hold a basket on his head as
in Davies' copy; the Ashmolean text is very abraded at this point.

79

CONCORDANCES AND INDEXES

1. Davies & Macadam, *Corpus.*

D.M. no.	Serial no.	D.M. no.	Serial no.	D.M. no.	Serial no.
3	127	110	10	217	28
4	38	112	2	221	119
5	50	123	20	228	64
6	125	124	21	230	117
7	60	125	115	232	100
9	148	126	116	245	92
13	109	127	98	246	63
15	52	133	128	247	130
22	39	134	161	249	141
24	40	138	138	255	155
26	56	139	139	257	47
37	154	144	133	260	37
39	149	151	22	263	48
41	73	153	108	264	69
43	9	158	131	265	15
45	41	162	23	270	6
46	18	164	24	271	46
54	103	168	66	277	110
55	89	170	88	288	29
62	111	172	34	294	49
64	43	173	137	298	99
73	14	180	53	301	105
74	19	181	146	304	16
76	32	185	25	306	51
87	94	189	44	308	159
89	95	192	26	309	118
92	36	193	101	311	153
94	1	204	7	312	136
97	83	206	74	313	151
100	75	210	27	320	135
103	4	212	71	321	17
107	106	215	143	334	61
109	91	216	104	339	152

D.M. no.	Serial no.	D.M. no.	Serial no.	D.M. no.	Serial no.
341	121	452	90	520	158
354	30	465	67	523	5
360	3	466	129	524	123
363	33	468	112	534	65
368	11	469	113	547	55
378	42	477	147	550	96
383	68	479	139	552	13
388	76	480	58	554	8
390	84	485	80	561	150
397	45	486	81	562	126
400	85	493	77	567	144
405	102	494	134	571	140
406	156	500	142	573	145
414	12	501	132	581	87
415	157	503	70	583	54
418	78	504	97	587	72
419	79	505	86	590	62
430	59	506	107	597	31
438	122	508	160	604	82
441	114	509	124	611	93
450	57	515	120		

2. U.C. Registration Numbers.

U.C. no.	Serial no.	U.C. no.	Serial no.	U.C. no.	Serial no.
30174	44	37527-45	56	37567-8	32
30181	57	37546	154	37569	94
30182	21	37547-9	149	37570	95
37510-1	127	37550	73	37571-2	36
37512	38	37551	9	37573-6	1
37513	50	37552-5	41	37577	83
37514-5	125	37556	18	37578-83	75
37516	60	37557-9	103	37584	4
37517-20	148	37560	89	37585	106
37521	109	37561-3	111	37586	91
37522-4	52	37564	43	37587	10
37525	39	37565	14	37588	2
37526	40	37566	19	37589	20

U.C. no.	Serial no.	U.C. no.	Serial no.	U.C. no.	Serial no.
37590-1	21	37681-3	15	37840	112
37592-3	115	37684-9	6	37841-2	113
37594-5	116	37690-		37843-5	147
37596	98	37730	46	37846	139
37597	128	37731	110	37847-52	58
37598-		37732	29	37853	80
37600	138	37733-4	49	37854	81
37601-2	139	37735	99	37855	77
37603	133	37736	105	37856	134
37604	22	37737-8	16	37857	142
37605-11	108	37739-49	51	37858-9	132
37612-5	131	37750-3	159	37860-1	70
37616	23	37754	118	37862-70	97
37617	24	37755-7	153	37871-3	86
37618-9	66	37758-9	136	37874	107
37620-33	88	37760-1	151	37875-37942	160
37634-7	34	37762-3	135	37943	124
37638-9	137	37764	17	37944	120
37640	53	37765-6	61	37945	158
37641	146	37767	152	37946	5
37642	25	37768	121	37947-53	123
37643	44	37769	30	37954-6	65
37644	26	37770	3	37957	55
37645-7	101	37771	33	37958-9	96
37648	74	37772-4	11	37960-1	13
37649-50	27	37775-6	42	37962	8
37651-2	71	37777-84	68	37963-4	150
37653	143	37785-8	76	37965-6	126
37654-5	104	37789-99	84	37967	144
37656-7	28	37800-1	45	37968-70	140
37658	119	37802-15	85	37971	145
37659	64	37816-7	102	37972	87
37660-1	117	37818	156	37973	54
37662-5	100	37819	12	37974	72
37666-70	92	37820-1	157	37975	62
37671	63	37822	78	37976	31
37672-3	130	37823	79	37977	82
37674	141	37824-7	59	37978	93
37675	155	37828	122	37979-80	88
37676	47	37829	114	37981	50
37677	37	37830	90	37987	161
37678-9	48	37831-8	67	37990-1	76
37680	69	37839	129	37992	7

3. Attributions to Theban tombs.

Tomb no.	Serial no.	Tomb no.	Serial no.	Tomb no.	Serial no.
11	47-8	92	146	249	108
29	15	95	84-5	279	112-3
34	78-82	97	9	297	14
36	57	108	99	343	114
41	17	109	91	344	125
47	156	123	11	346	123
48	147	127	134	367	117
55	128	132	127	383	88
66	54	150	155	398	109
79	76-7	155	139	A.1	10
81	58	196	120	A.3	131
85	6	200	38-40	A.6	45
86	75	201	129	A.8	8
87	94-5	224	1		

4. Royal names.

Amenophis I, 7.
Amenophis II, 103.
Amenophis III, 59.
Sheshonq IV, 56.
Tuthmosis I, 4, 122.
Tuthmosis II, 100, 101.
Tuthmosis III, 62, 64.

Note on the Plates

Much of the decoration reproduced here, whether photographically or by drawings, is from surfaces which are in relief, and may be subject to some distortion. In the drawings this has been confined as much as possible to the intervening spaces. Where linear scales are not applicable, the main dimensions may be obtained from the descriptive text.

Plate 2   2,3. Fragments of rectangular coffins.

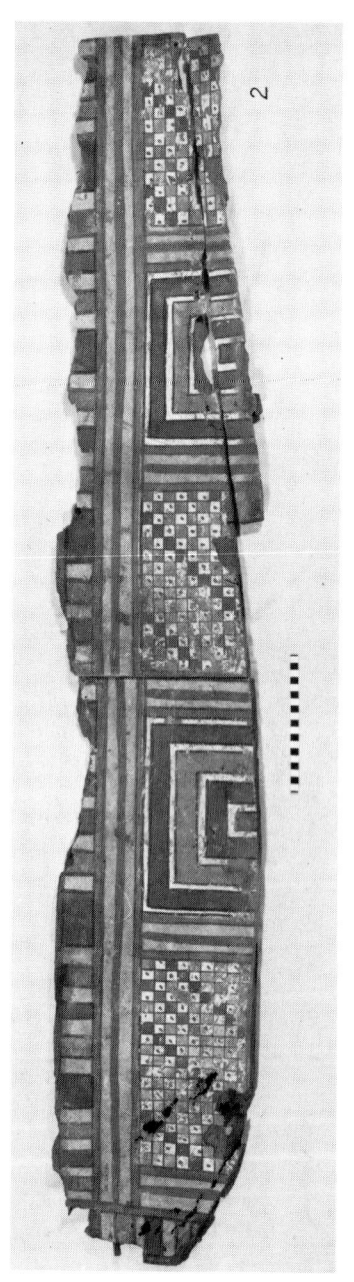

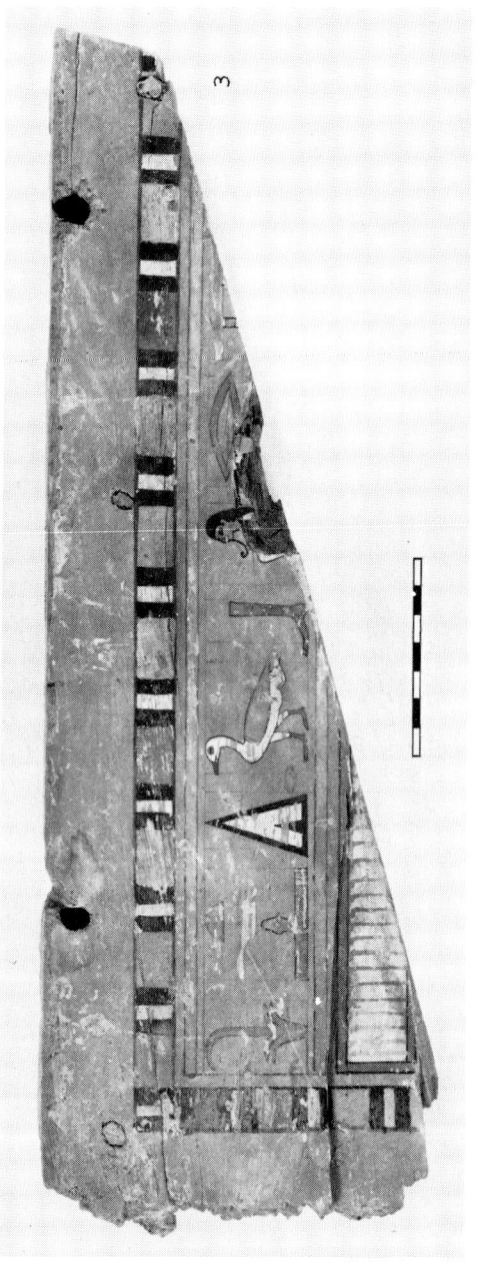

Plate 4   4. Upper part of lid

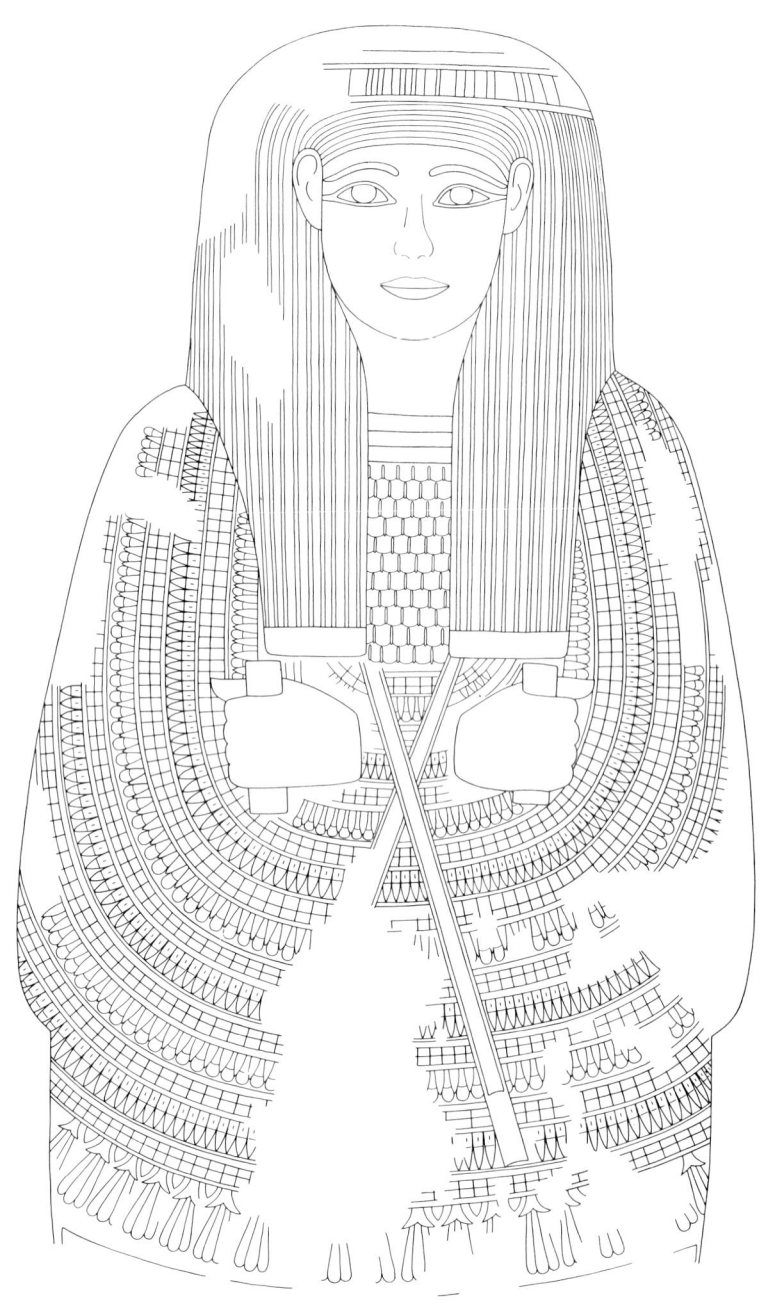

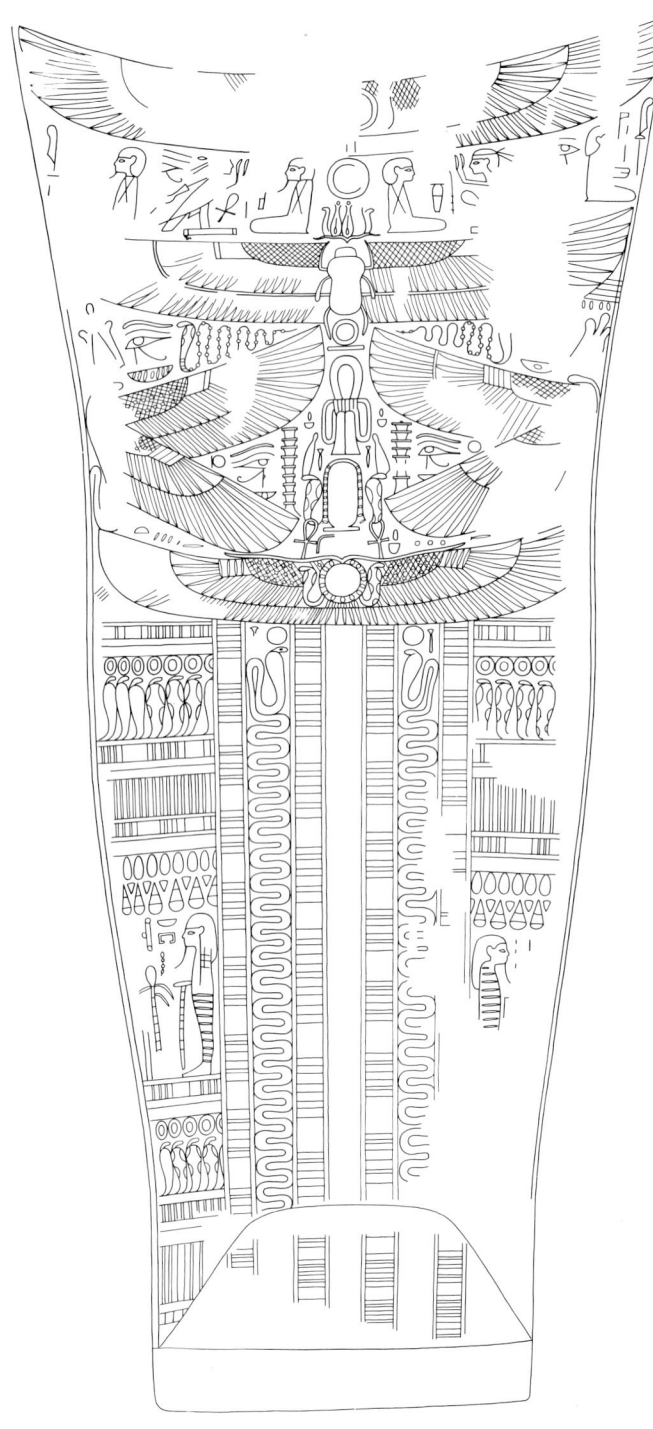

4. Left side of base.

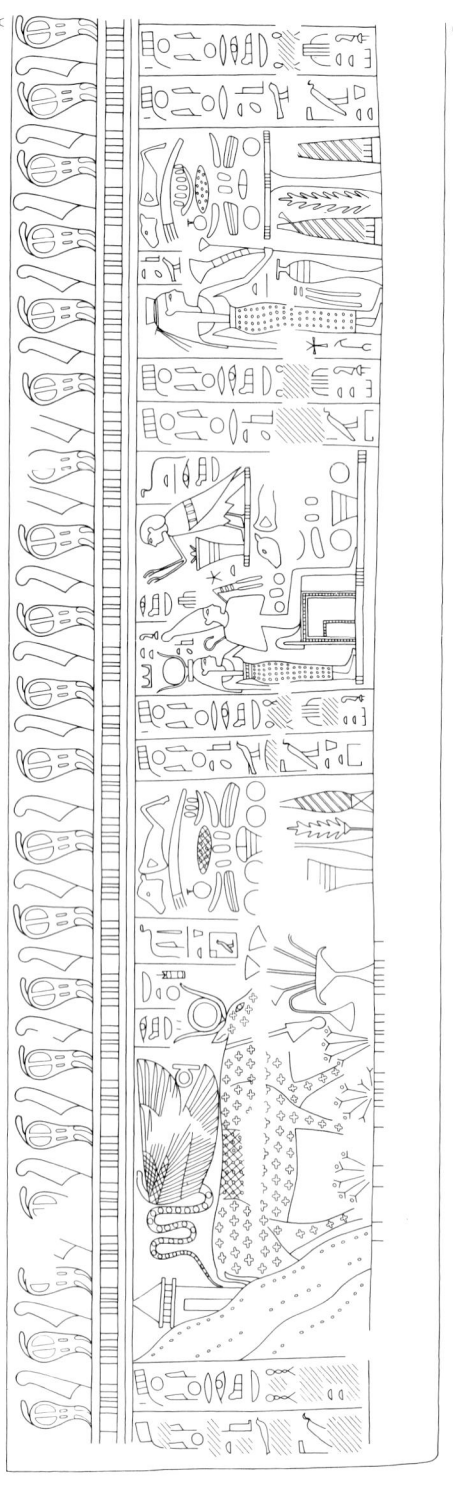

Plate 5

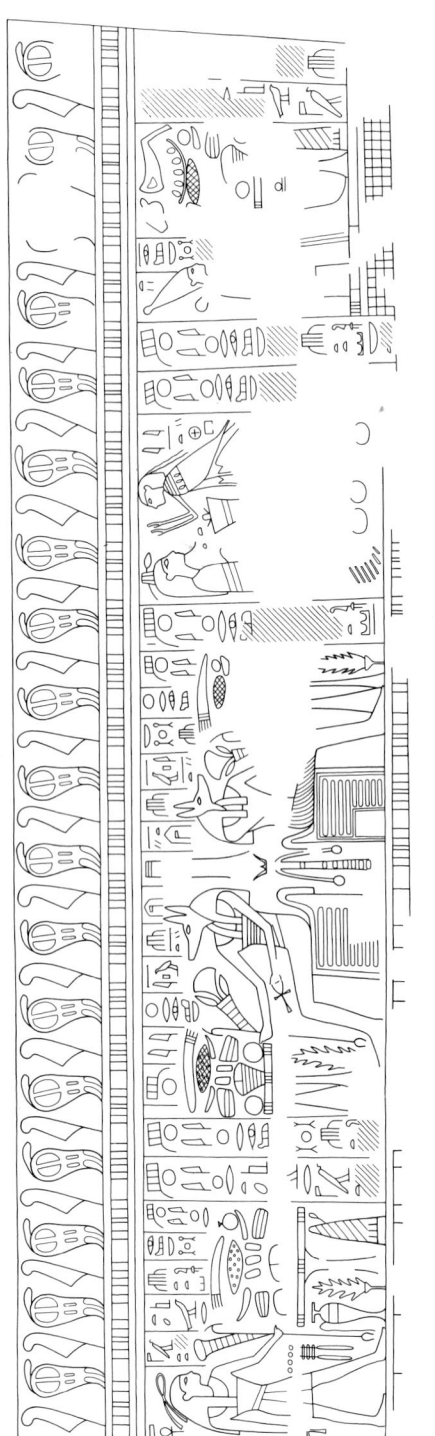

4. Right side of base.

Plate 6

Plate 7   4. Floor of interior

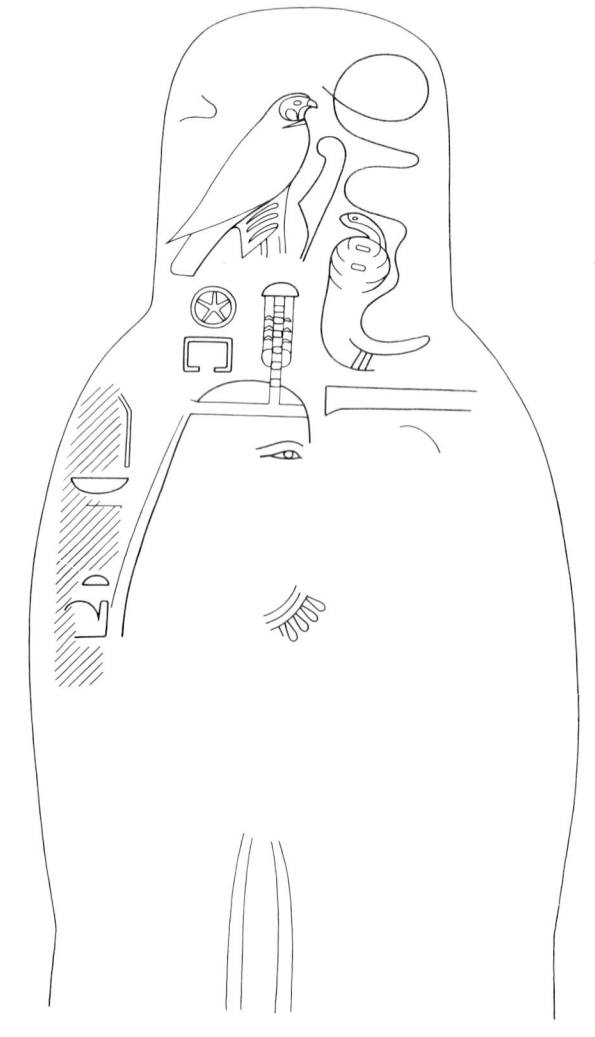

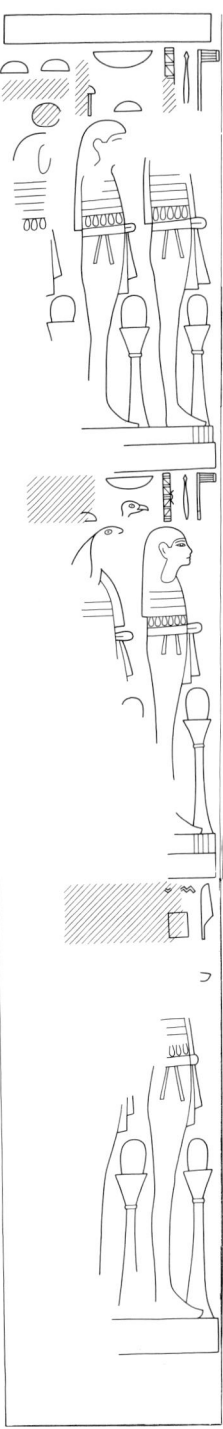

Plate 9   5. Coffin of Amenemopet. Fragment, exterior

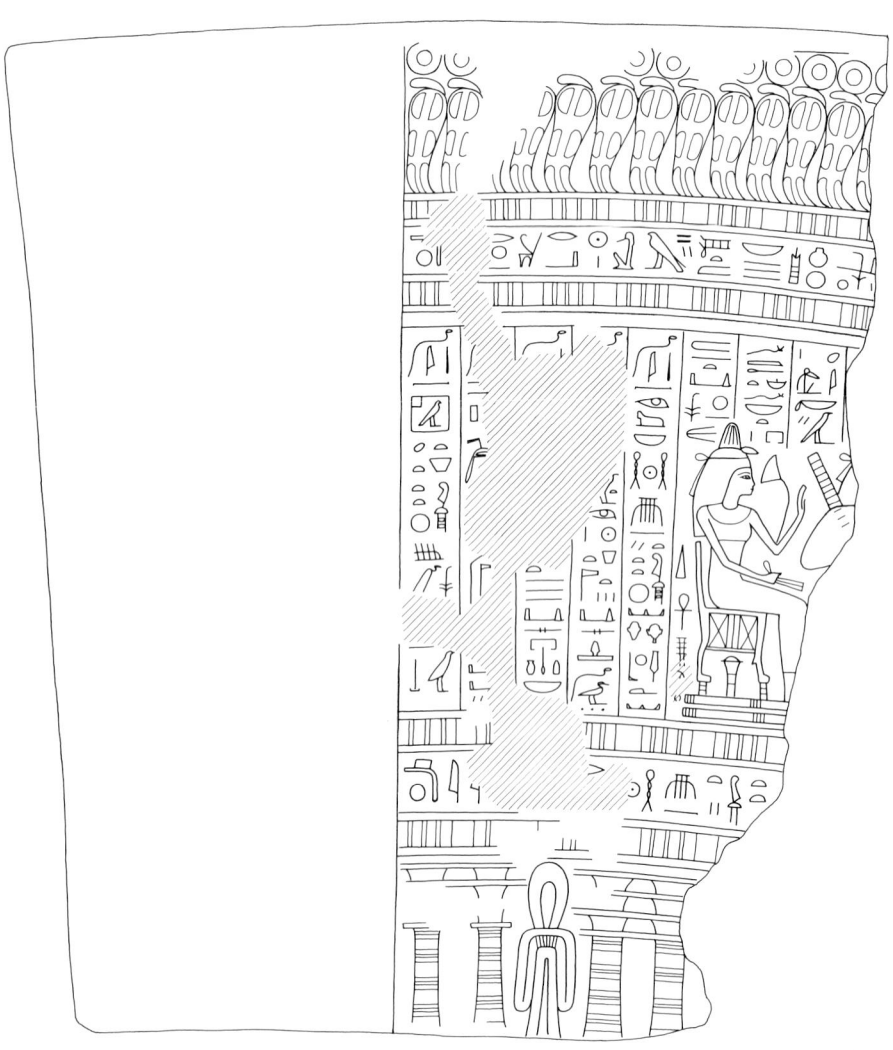

Plate 11   6. Fragment of anthropoid coffin, exterior
9-13. Fragments of cartonnage.

6

9

10

11

12

13

0   10 cm.

Plate 13   7. Upper part of lid, exterior

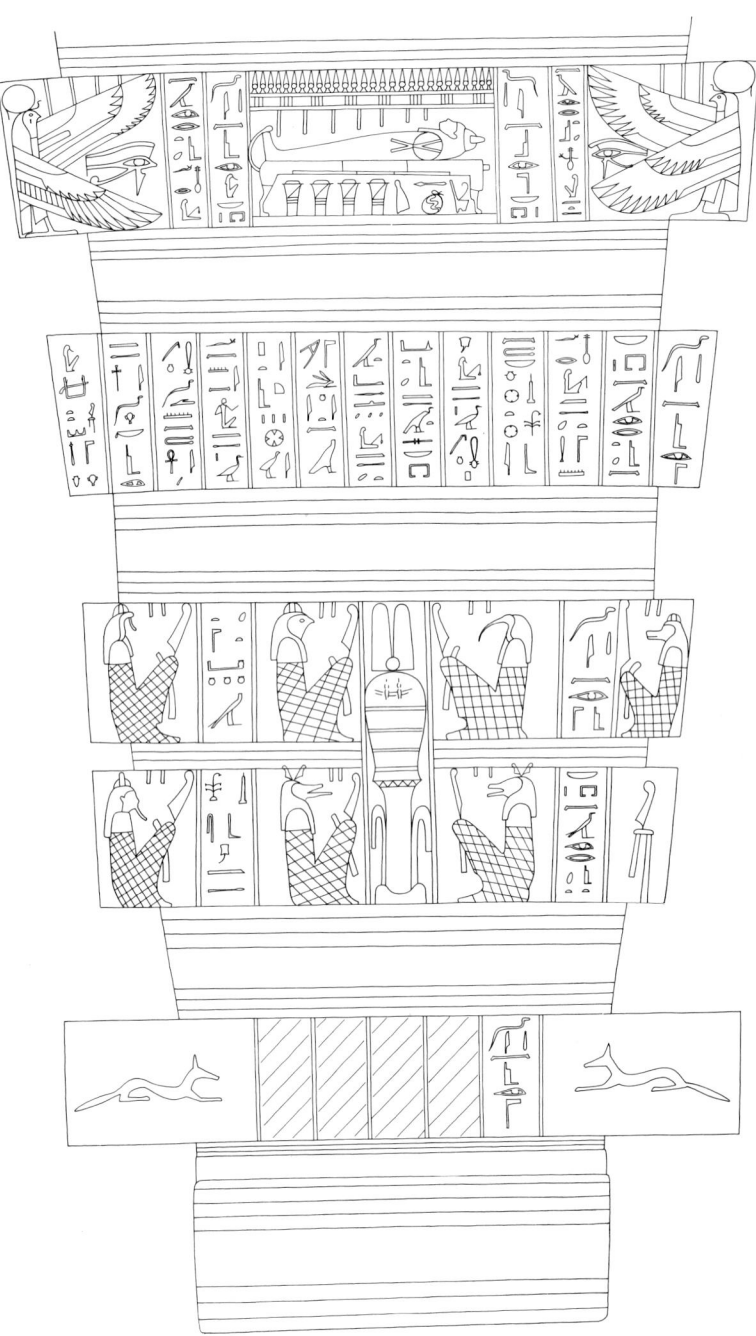

Plate 14   7. Upper part of base, exterior

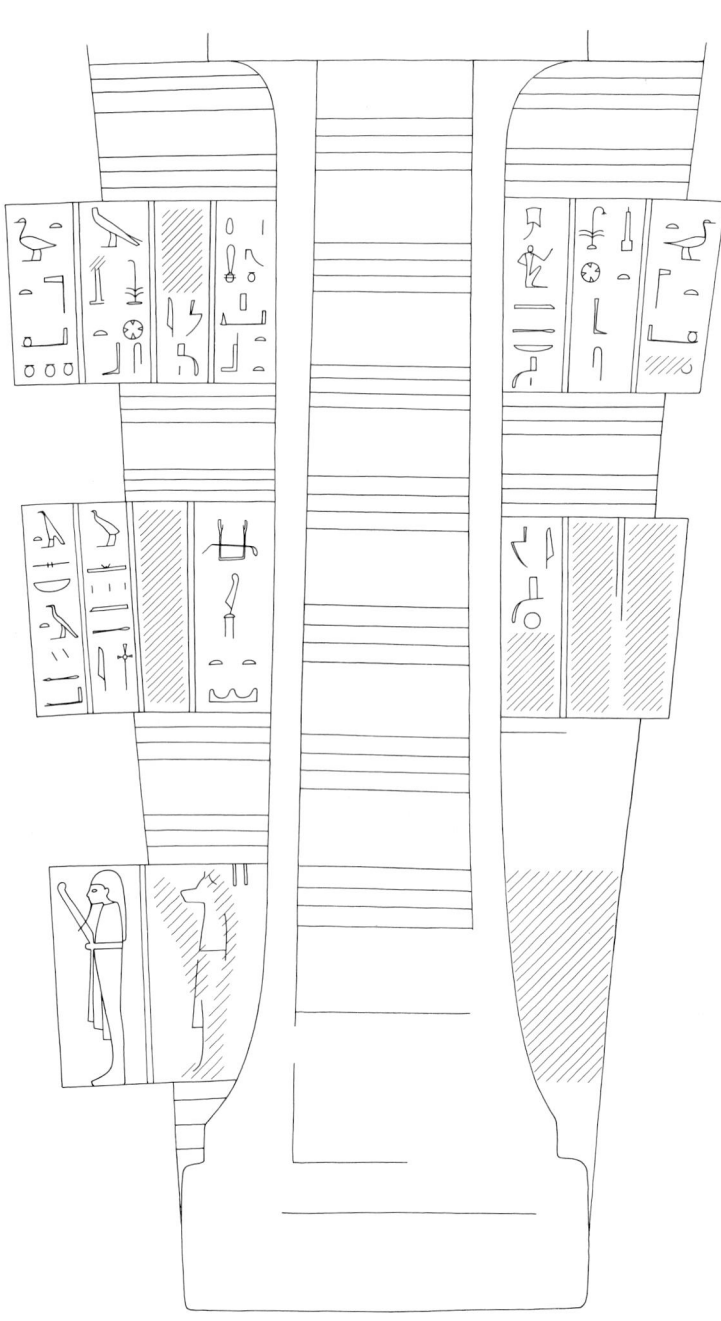

Plate 15   7. Upper part of lid, interior

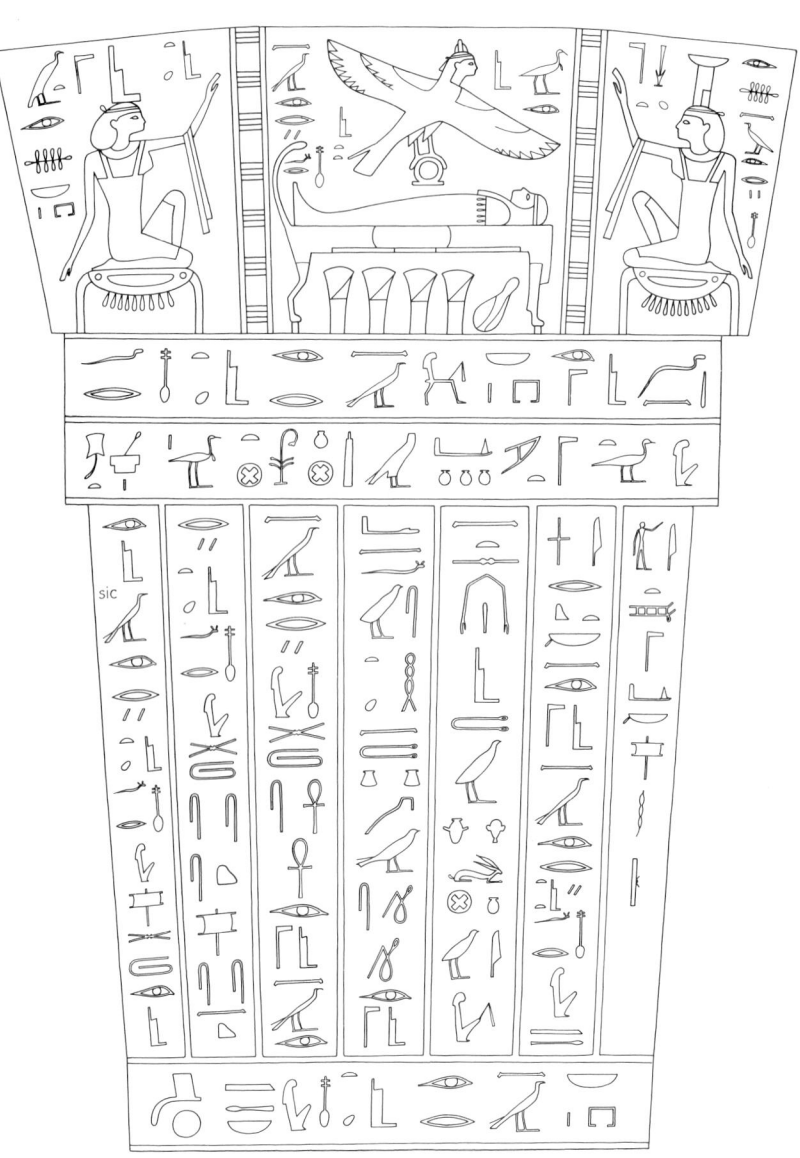

Plate 16   7. Upper part of base, interior

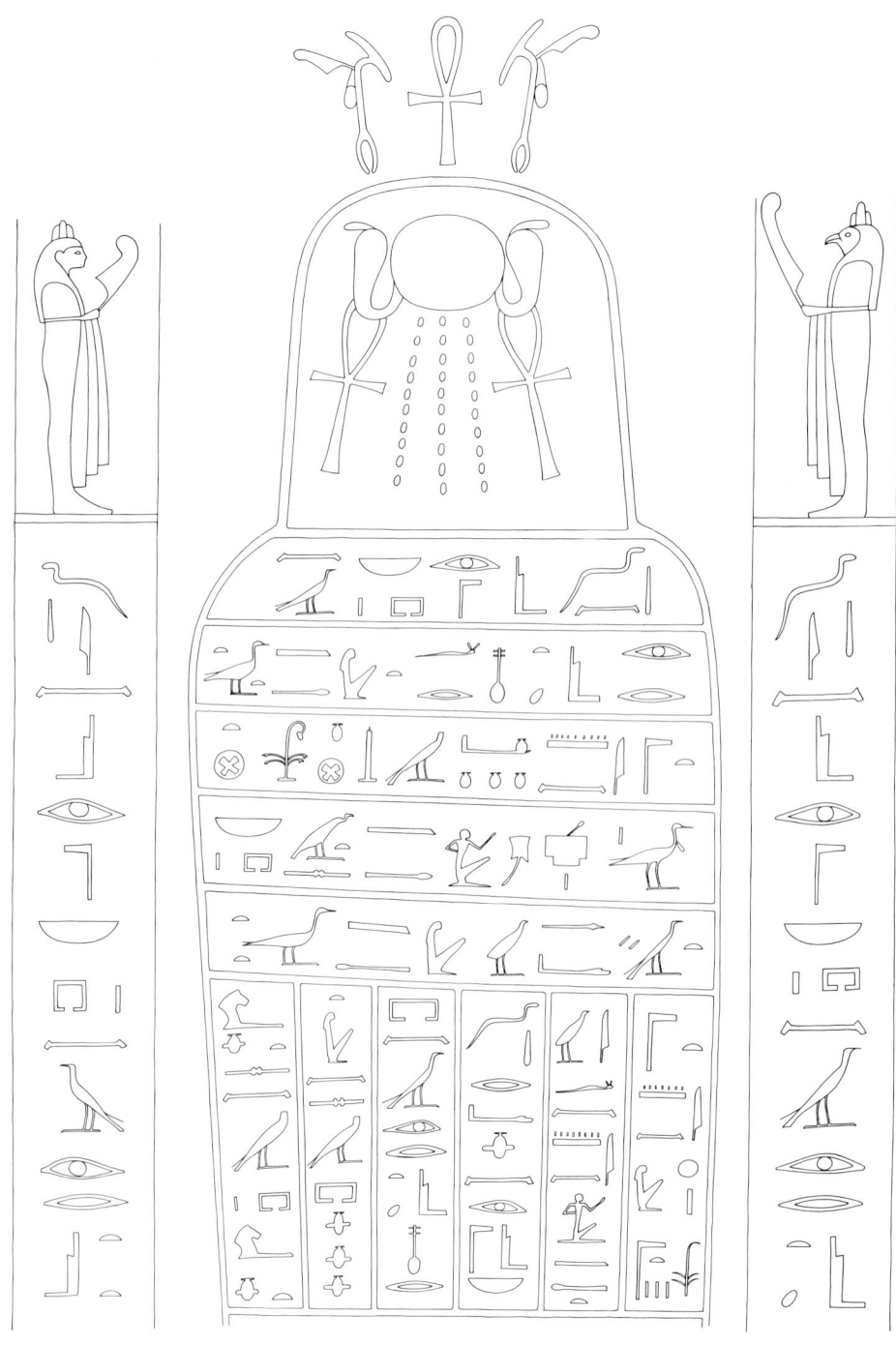

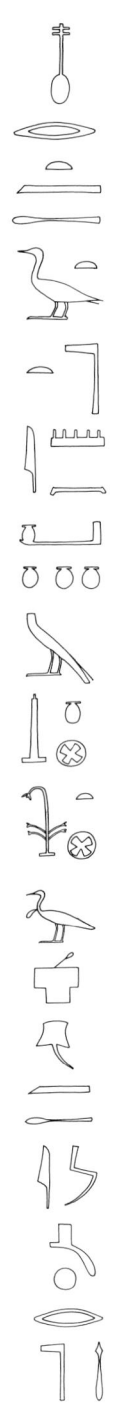

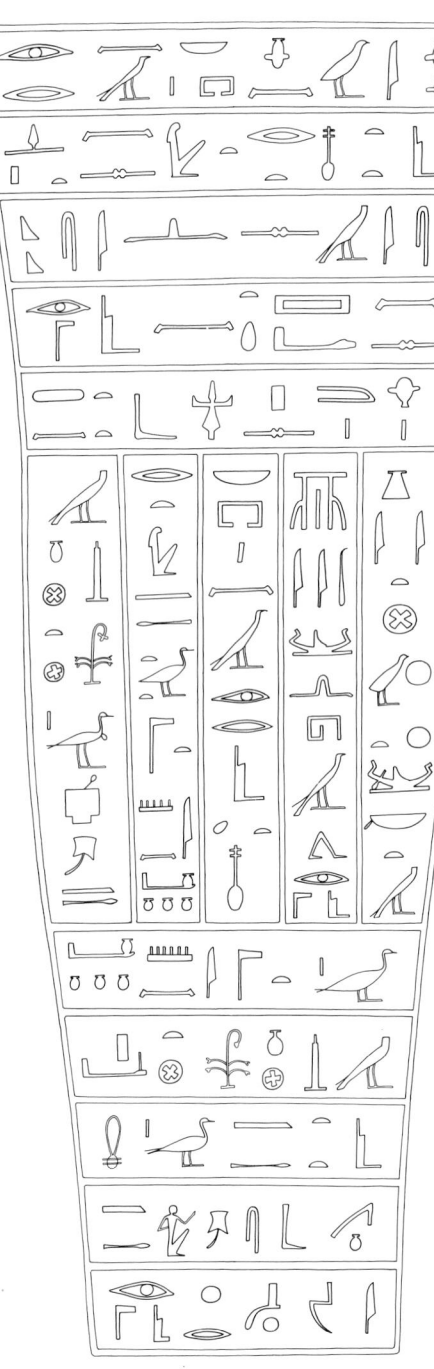

Plate 17   8. Fragment, cartonnage of Nespautitawy

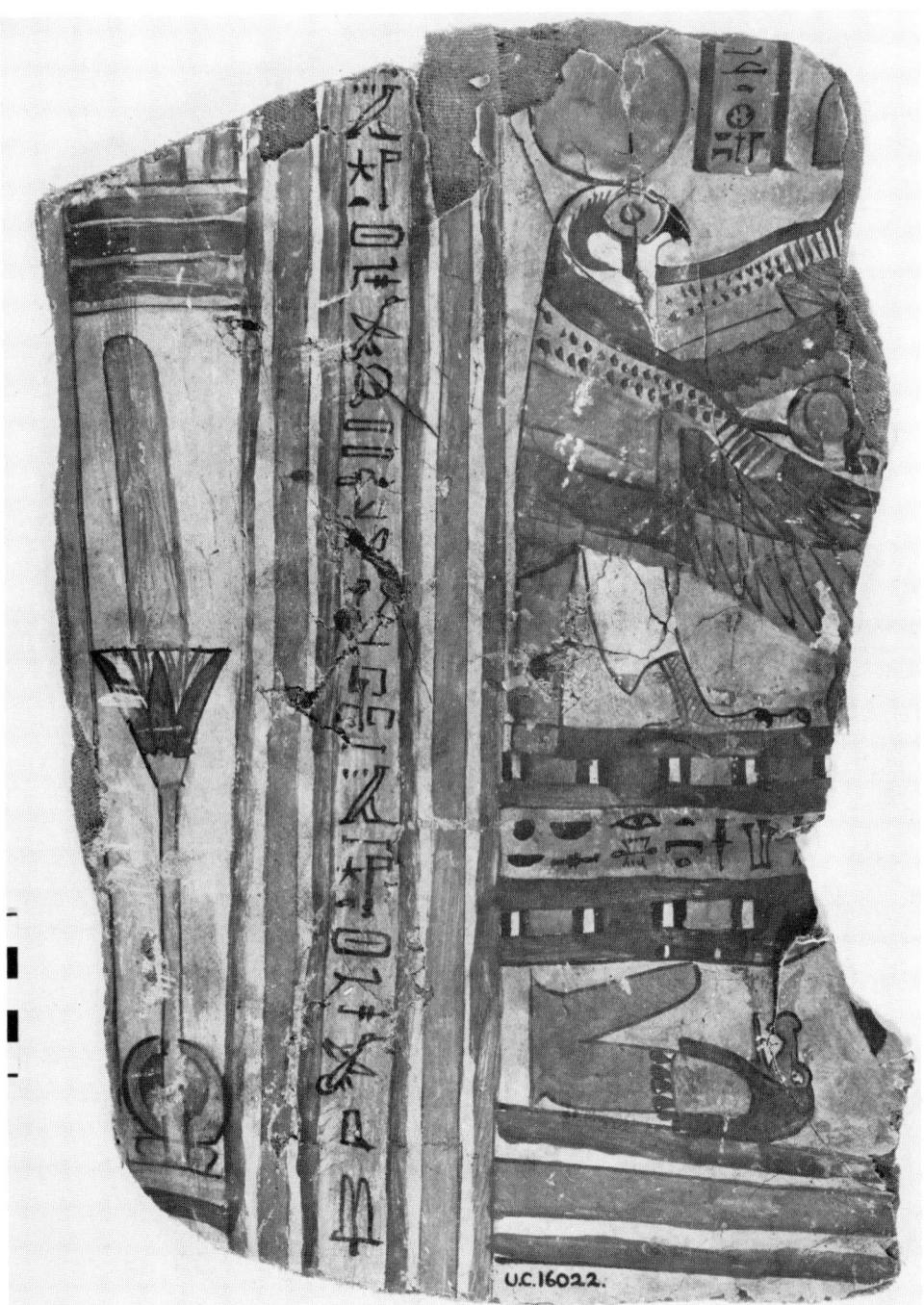

U.C.16022.

Plate 19   14. Cartonnage of Pediamun-nesuttawy

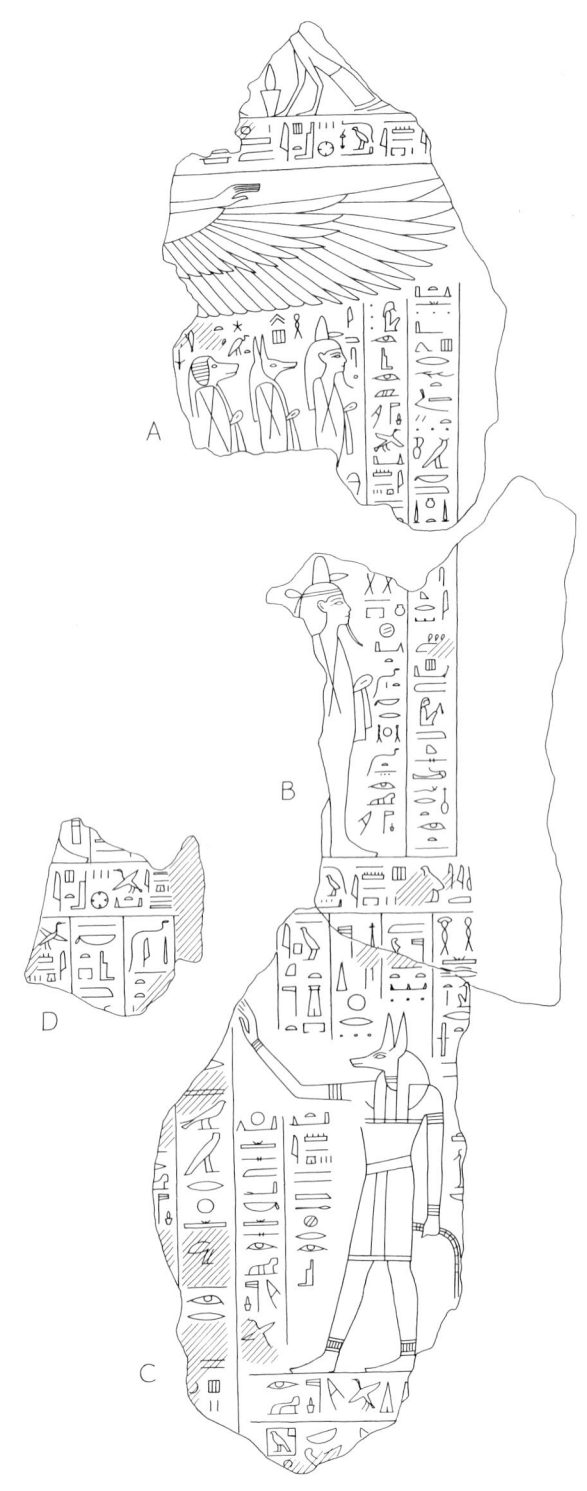

Plate 21   16. Cartonnage mask

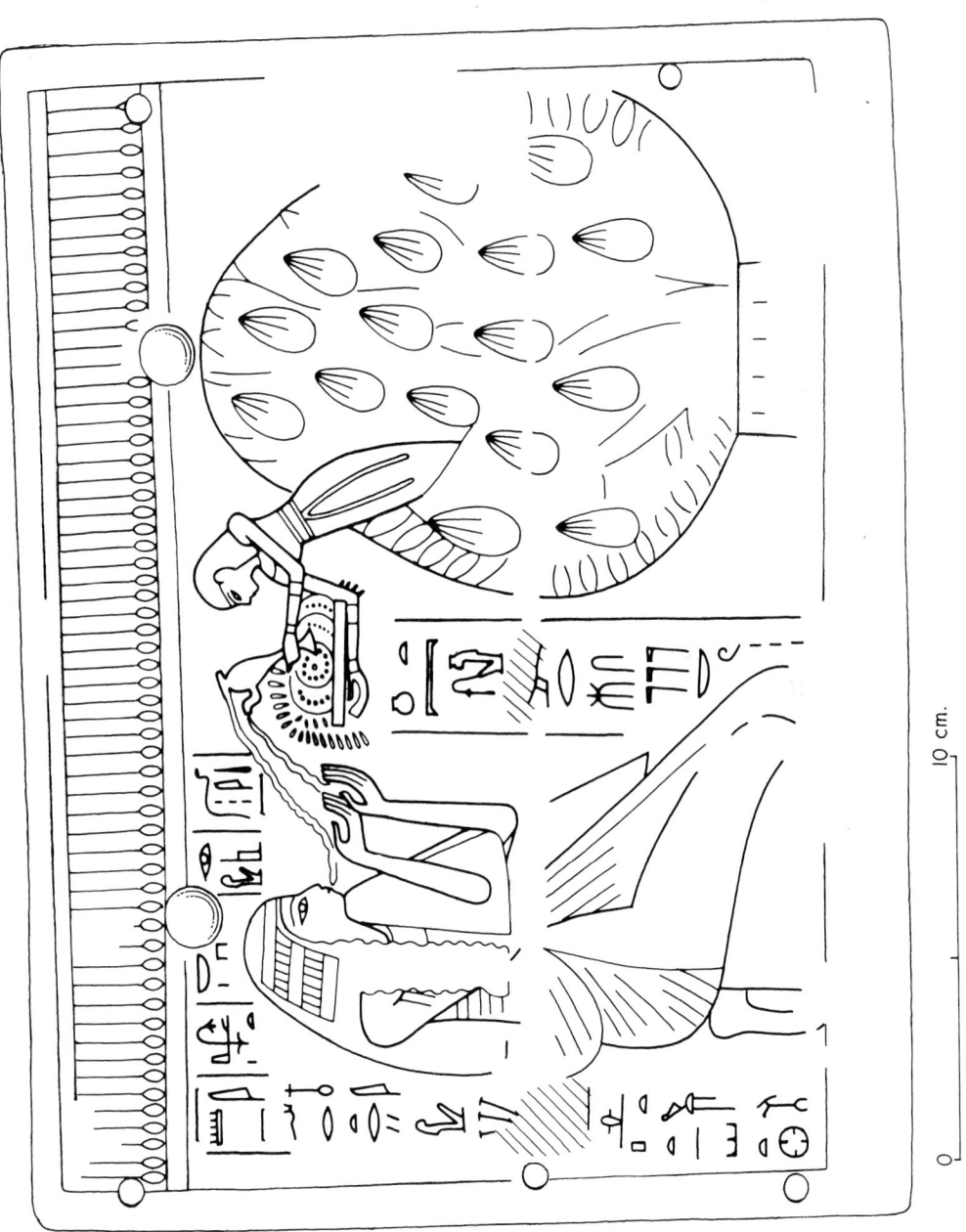

10 cm.

Plate 23   18. Shabti box of Basa

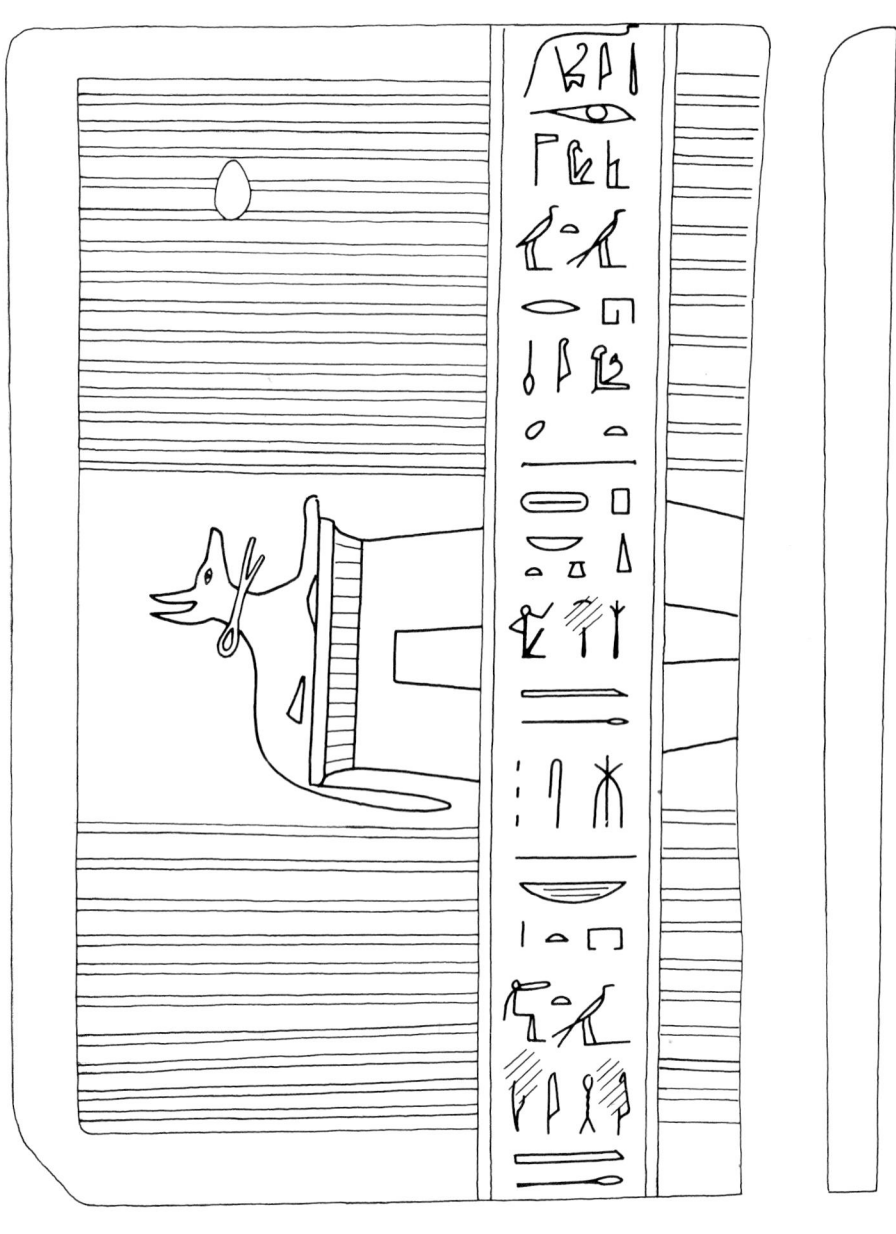

0 _____ 10 cm.

Plate 25   Inscribed pottery cones

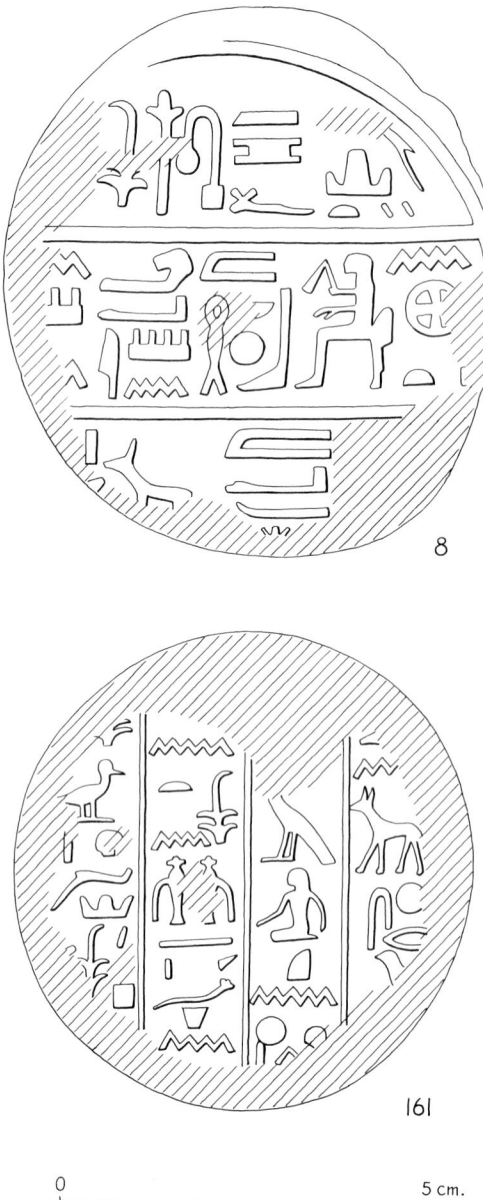

8

161

0 ⊢——————————————⊣ 5 cm.